SIMPLY IN DEPTH

MPICH
PROGRAMMING

PARALLEL COMPUTING

AJIT SINGH
PROF BAL GANGADHAR PRASAD

ISBN-13: 9781983353420

ACKNOWLEDGEMENT

This piece of study of **Parallel Computing** is an outcome of the encouragement, guidance, help and assistance provided to us by our colleagues, Sr. faculties, Tech-friends and our family members.

As an acknowledgement, we would like to take the opportunity to express our deep sense of gratitude to all those who played a crucial role in the successful completion of this book, especially to our sr. students; this book certainly has been benefited from discussions held with many IT professionals (Ex-students) over the years it took us to write it.

Our primary goal here was to provide a sufficient introduction and details of the **Parallel Computing** so that the students can have an efficient knowledge about **Parallel Computing**. Moreover, it presupposes knowledge of the principles and concepts of the C and FORTAN languages are required. On the same note, any errors and inaccuracies are our responsibility and any suggestions in this regard are warmly welcomed!

Finally, we would like to thank the **Kindle Direct Publishing** team and **Amazon** team for its enthusiastic online support and guidance in bringing out this book.

We hope that the reader will like this book and find it useful in learning the concepts of **Parallel Computing** with practical implementation of MPI.

Thank You !!

Ajit Singh & Prof Dr B. G. Prasad

PREFACE

Share the knowledge,

Strengthen the surrounding......!!!

The study/learning of **Parallel Computing** is an essential part of any computer science education and of course for the B.Tech / MCA / M.Tech courses of several Universities across the world. This textbook is intended as a guide for an explanatory course of **Parallel Computing** for the Graduate and Post Graduate Students of several universities across the world.

To The Student

This text is an introduction to the complex and emerging world of the **Parallel Computing**. It helps you understand the principles and acquire the practical skills of MPI programming using the C/FORTAN programming language. Our aim is for you to gain sufficient knowledge and experience to perform simple useful programming tasks using the best up-to-date techniques and so we hope for it to be the easiest book from which you can learn the basics of MPI programming.

This text is an introduction to the emerging world of the Parallel Computing. It helps you understand the principles, algorithm & implementation of Parallel Computing. Our aim is for you to gain sufficient knowledge and experience with Parallel Computing using the best up-to-date techniques. We have tried for it to be the easiest book from which you can learn the Parallel Computing.

We chose the topics for this book to cover what is needed to get started with Parallel Computing, not just what is easy to teach and learn. On the other hand, we won't waste your time with material of marginal practical importance. If an idea is explained here, it's because you'll almost certainly need it.

This book is emphatically focused on "the concept". Understanding the fundamental ideas, principles, and techniques is the essence of a good programmer. Only well-designed code has a chance of becoming part of a correct, reliable, and maintainable parallel system. Through this book, we hope that you will see the absolute necessity of understanding Parallel Computing.

3

Feedback

We have attempted to wash out every error in our first edition of this book after being reviewed by lots of scholars of Computer Science, but as happens with MPI Programming – "A few bugs difficult to understand shall remain" – and therefore, suggestions from students that may lead to improvement of next edition in shortcoming future are highly appreciated.

*Conclusive suggestions and criticism always go a long way in enhancing any endeavour. We request all readers to email us their valuable comments / views / feedback for the betterment of the book at **ajit_singh24@yahoo.com / profbgprasad@gmail.com** mentioning the title and author name in the subject line. Please report any piracy spotted by you as well . We would be glad to hear suggestions from you.*

We hope, you enjoy reading this book as much as we have enjoyed writing it. We would be glad to hear suggestions from you.

About the Author(s)

Ajit Singh

Ajit is currently a Ph.D candidate at Magadh University, Bihar, IND working on Social Media Predictive Data Analytics at the A. N. College Research Centre, Patna, IND, under the supervision of *Prof Dr Manish Kumar* (Associate Professor-Dept of Mathematics, A. N. College, MU, Bihar).
He also holds M.Phil. degree in Computer Science, and is a Microsoft MCSE / MCDBA / MCSD.. His main interests are in algorithm, programming languages and Operating Systems.

Ajit can be contacted via one of two places:
http://facebook.com/ajitseries
http://amazon.com/author/ajitsingh

Email: *ajit_singh24@yahoo.com*
Ph: +91-92-346-11498

Dr. Prof Bal Gangadhar Prasad
HOD-Department of Mathematics (PG)
Patna University, Bihar, IND
Mobile - 8294302791
Email: profbgprasad@gmail.com

CONTENTS

Sl No	Topic(s)	Pg No
1	**INTRODUCTION TO PARALLEL COMPUTING**	8
	Introduction	
	Background	
	Problem Solving in Parallel	
	Concept of Temporal Parallelism	
	Concept of Data Parallelism	
	Functional Parallelism	
	Classes of parallel computers	
	Performance Evaluation	
	The Concept of Concurrent and Parallel Execution	
	Granularity	
	Potential of Parallelism	
	Data Clustering	
	Minsky Conjecture	
	The Need of Parallel Computation	
	Levels of Parallel Processing	
	Bit Level	
	Instruction Level	
	Loop Level	
	Procedure Level	
	Program Level	
	Applications of Parallel Processing	
	Scientific Applications/Image Processing	
	Engineering Applications	
	Database Query/Answering Systems	
	AI Applications	
	Mathematical Simulation and Modeling Applications	
	Supercomputers and grand challenge problems	
	Modem Parallel Computers	
	Future of parallel computing	
2	**CLASSIFICATION OF PARALLEL COMPUTERS**	23
	Introduction	
	Types of Classification	
	Flynn's Classification	
	Instruction Cycle	
	Instruction Stream and Data Stream	
	Flynn's Classification	
	Handler's Classification	
	Structural Classification	
	Shared Memory System/Tightly Coupled System	
	Uniform Memory Access Model	
	Non-Uniform Memory Access Model	
	Cache-only Memory Architecture Model	
	Loosely Coupled Systems	

	Classification Based on Grain Size Parallelism Conditions Bernstein Conditions for Detection of Parallelism Parallelism Based on Grain Size	
3	**INTERCONNECTION NETWORK** Introduction Network Properties Design issues of Interconnection Network Various Interconnection Networks Concept of Permutation Network Performance Metrics	37
4	**PARALLEL COMPUTER ARCHITECTURE** Introduction Pipeline Processing Classification of Pipeline Processors Instruction Pipelines Arithmetic Pipelines Performance and Issues in Pipelining Vector Processing Array Processing Associative Array Processing Multi-threaded Processors	53
5	**PERFORMANCE ANALYSIS OF PARALLEL COMPUTING** Introduction Definitions Performance analysis Performance analysis techniques Performance analysis metrics Efficiency Speedup Amdahl's Law Gustafson Law Gustafson-Barsis's Law Superlinear Speedup and Efficiency The Karp-Flatt Metric The Isoefficiency Metric Isoefficiency Relation Cost and Scalability	69
6	**PARALLEL COMPUTATIONAL MODEL** PRAM CRCW CREW EREW, Simulating CRCW on CREW & SREW PRAM algorithms	90

	P-Complete problems.	
7	**INTRODUCTION TO PARALLEL ALGORITHMS** PVM MPI Paradigms Simple parallel programs in MPI/PVM environments Parallel algorithms on network Addition of Matrices Multiplication of Matrices Parallel Programming Issues Systolic Array	98

1

INTRODUCTION TO PARALLEL COMPUTING

Introduction
Background
Problem Solving in Parallel
Concept of Temporal Parallelism
Concept of Data Parallelism
Functional Parallelism
Classes of parallel computers
Performance Evaluation
The Concept of Concurrent and Parallel Execution
    Granularity
    Potential of Parallelism
Pipelining and Data Clustering
Minsky Conjecture
The Need of Parallel Computation
Levels of Parallel Processing
    Bit Level
    Instruction Level
    Loop Level
    Procedure Level
    Program Level
Applications of Parallel Processing
    Scientific Applications/Image Processing
    Engineering Applications
    Database Query/Answering Systems
    AI Applications
    Mathematical Simulation and Modeling Applications
Future of parallel computing

INTRODUCTION

Parallel computing has been a subject of interest in the computing community over the last few decades. Ever-growing size of databases and increasing complexity of the new problems are putting great stress on the even the super-fast modern single processor computers. Now the entire computer science community all over the world is looking for some computing environment where current computational capacity can be enhanced by a factor in order of thousands. The most obvious solution is the introduction of multiple processors working in tandem i.e. the introduction of parallel computing.

Parallel computing is a form of computation in which many calculations are carried out simultaneously, operating on the principle that large problems can often be divided into smaller ones, which are then solved concurrently ("in parallel").

Parallel computing is the simultaneous execution of the same task, split into subtasks, on multiple processors in order to obtain results faster. The idea is based on the fact that the process of solving a problem can usually be divided into smaller tasks, which may be solved out simultaneously with some coordination mechanisms. Before going into the details of parallel computing, we shall discuss some basic concepts frequently used in parallel computing.

Then we shall explain why we require parallel computing and what the levels of parallel processing are. We shall see how flow of data occurs in parallel processing. We shall conclude this unit with a discussion of role the of parallel processing in some fields like science and engineering, database queries and artificial intelligence.

BACKGROUND

Traditionally, computer software has been written for serial computation. To solve a problem, an algorithm is constructed and implemented as a serial stream of instructions. These instructions are executed on a central processing unit on one computer. Only one instruction may execute at a time—after that instruction is finished, the next is executed.

Parallel computing, on the other hand, uses multiple processing elements simultaneously to solve a problem. This is accomplished by breaking the problem into independent parts so that each processing element can execute its part of the algorithm simultaneously with the others. The processing elements can be diverse and include resources such as a single computer with multiple processors, several networked computers, specialized hardware, or any combination of the above.

The experiments with and implementations of the use of parallelism started long back in the 1950s by the IBM. The IBM STRETCH computers also known as IBM 7030 were built in 1959. In the design of these computers, a number of new concepts like overlapping I/O with processing and instruction look ahead were introduced. A serious approach towards designing parallel computers was started with the development of ILLIAC IV in 1964 at the University of Illionis. It had a single control unit but multiple processing elements. On this machine, at one time, a single operation is executed on different data items by different processing elements. The concept of pipelining was introduced in computer CDC 7600 in 1969. It used pipelined arithmatic unit. In the years 1970 to 1985, the research in this area was focused on the development of vector super computer. In 1976, the CRAY1 was developed by Seymour Cray. Cray1 was a pioneering effort in the development of vector registers. It accessed main memory only for load and store operations. Cray1 did not use virtual memory, and optimized pipelined arithmetic unit. Cray1 had clock speed of 12.5 n.sec. The Cray1 processor evolved upto a speed of 12.5 Mflops on 100×100 linear equation solutions. The next generation of Cray called Cray XMP was developed in the years 1982-84. It was coupled with 8-vector supercomputers and used a shared memory.

Frequency scaling was the dominant reason for improvements in computer performance from the mid-1980s until 2004. The runtime of a program is equal to the number of instructions multiplied by the average time per instruction. Maintaining everything else constant, increasing the clock frequency decreases the average time it takes to execute an instruction. An increase in frequency thus decreases runtime for all compute-bound programs.

PROBLEM SOLVING IN PARALLEL

This section discusses how a given task can be broken into smaller subtasks and how subtasks can be solved in parallel. However, it is essential to note that there are certain applications which are inherently sequential and if for such applications, a parallel computer is used then the performance does not improve.

Concept of Temporal Parallelism

In order to explain what is meant by parallelism inherent in the solution of a problem, let us discuss an example of submission of electricity bills. Suppose there are 10000 residents in a locality and they are supposed to submit their electricity bills in one office.

Let us assume the steps to submit the bill are as follows:
Go to the appropriate counter to take the form to submit the bill.
Submit the filled form along with cash.
Get the receipt of submitted bill.

Assume that there is only one counter with just single office person performing all the tasks of giving application forms, accepting the forms, counting the cash, returning the cash if the need be, and giving the receipts.

This situation is an example of sequential execution. Let us the approximate time taken by various of events be as follows:

Giving application form = 5 seconds
Accepting filled application form and counting the cash and returning, if required = 5mnts, i.e., 5 ×60= 300 sec.
Giving receipts = 5 seconds.
Total time taken in processing one bill = 5+300+5 = 310 seconds.

Now, if we have 3 persons sitting at three different counters with
One person giving the bill submission form
One person accepting the cash and returning,if necessary and
One person giving the receipt.

The time required to process one bill will be 300 seconds because the first and third activity will overlap with the second activity which takes 300 sec. whereas the first and last activity take only 10 secs each. This is an example of a parallel processing method as here 3 persons work in parallel. As three persons work in the same time, it is called temporal parallelism. However, this is a poor example of parallelism in the sense that one of the actions i.e., the second action takes 30 times of the time taken by each of the other two actions. The word 'temporal' means 'pertaining to time'. Here, a task is broken into many subtasks, and those subtasks are executed simultaneously in the time domain. In terms of computing application it can be said that parallel computing is possible, if it is possible, to break the computation or problem in to identical independent computation. Ideally, for parallel processing, the task should be divisible into a number of activities, each of which take roughly same amount of time as other activities.

Concept of Data Parallelism

consider the situation where the same problem of submission of 'electricity bill' is handled as follows:
Again, three are counters. However, now every counter handles all the tasks of a resident in respect of submission of his/her bill. Again, we assuming that time required to submit one bill form is the same as earlier, i.e., 5+300+5=310 sec.

We assume all the counters operate simultaneously and each person at a counter takes 310 seconds to process one bill. Then, time taken to process all the 10,000 bills will be
310 ×(9999 / 3) +310 ×1sec.

This time is comparatively much less as compared to time taken in the earlier situations, viz. 3100000 sec. and 3000000 sec respectively.

The situation discussed here is the concept of data parallelism. In data parallelism, the complete set of data is divided into multiple blocks and operations on the blocks are applied parallelly. As is clear from this example, data parallelism is faster as compared to earlier situations. Here, no synchronisation is required between counters(or processors). It is more tolerant of faults. The working of one person does not effect the other. There is no communication required between processors. Thus, interprocessor communication is less. Data parallelism has certain disadvantages. These are as follows:

The task to be performed by each processor is predecided i.e., assignment of load is static.

It should be possible to break the input task into mutually exclusive tasks. In the given example, space would be required counters. This requires multiple hardware which may be costly.

The estimation of speedup achieved by using the above type of parallel processing is as follows:

Let the number of jobs = m
Let the time to do a job = p

If each job is divided into k tasks,
Assuming task is ideally divisible into activities, as mentioned above then,
Time to complete one task = p/k
Time to complete n jobs without parallel processing = n.p
Time to complete n jobs with parallel processing = (n * p) / k

$$\text{Speed up} = \frac{\text{time to complete the task if parallelism is not used}}{\text{time to complete the task if parallelism is used}}$$

$$= \frac{np}{n\dfrac{p}{k}}$$

$$= k$$

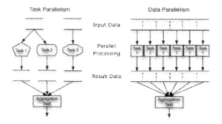

Concept of Functional Parallelism

This kind of parallelism is based on different functional blocks in your application. The idea is simple: The application is split into separate processing units, that communicate with a fixed number other units in such a way that the output of one part serves as the input of another part. Thus we can visualize such a system as a set of nodes that are connected by pipes in which data only flow in one direction.

A good example is a compiler. Such a compiler may consist of a scanner, a parser and a code-generator. The output of the scanner is the input of the parser. The output of the parser is the input of the code-generator. And the output of the code generator is written to the disk.

Each of these parts may be placed on a different processor.

Features:
- simple concept
- functional blocks are easy to identify
- low overhead
- simple communication structure (forward)

Problems:
- uneven processing times cause uneven processor loads
- number of processors is restricted (little scalability)
- no or restricted load balancing

CLASSES OF PARALLEL COMPUTERS

Parallel computers can be roughly classified according to the level at which the hardware supports parallelism. This classification is broadly analogous to the distance between basic computing nodes. These are not mutually exclusive; for example, clusters of symmetric multiprocessors are relatively common.

Multicore computing

A multicore processor is a processor that includes multiple execution units ("cores") on the same chip. These processors differ from superscalar processors, which can issue multiple instructions per cycle from one instruction stream (thread); in contrast, a multicore processor can issue multiple instructions per cycle from multiple instruction streams. IBM's Cell microprocessor, designed for use in the Sony PlayStation 3, is another prominent multicore processor.

Each core in a multicore processor can potentially be superscalar as well—that is, on every cycle, each core can issue multiple instructions from one instruction stream. Simultaneous multithreading (of which Intel's HyperThreading is the best known) was an early form of pseudo-multicoreism. A processor capable of simultaneous multithreading has only one execution unit ("core"), but when that execution unit is idling (such as during a cache miss), it uses that execution unit to process a second thread.

Symmetric multiprocessing

A symmetric multiprocessor (SMP) is a computer system with multiple identical processors that share memory and connect via a bus. Bus contention prevents bus architectures from scaling. As a result, SMPs generally do not comprise more than 32 processors. "Because of the small size of the processors and the significant reduction in the requirements for bus bandwidth achieved by large caches, such symmetric multiprocessors are extremely cost-effective, provided that a sufficient amount of memory bandwidth exists."

Distributed computing

A distributed computer (also known as a distributed memory multiprocessor) is a distributed memory computer system in which the processing elements are connected by a network. Distributed computers are highly scalable.
Distributed computing is the most distributed form of parallel computing. It makes use of computers communicating over the Internet to work on a given problem. Because of the low bandwidth and extremely high latency available on the Internet, distributed computing typically deals only with embarrassingly parallel problems. Many distributed computing applications have been created, of which SETI@home and Folding@home are the best-known examples.

Difference between Parallel and distributed computing

Distributed systems are groups of networked computers, which have the same goal for their work.
The terms "concurrent computing", "parallel computing", and "distributed computing" have a lot of overlap,
and no clear distinction exists between them.
The same system may be characterized both as "parallel" and "distributed"; the processors in a typical distributed system run concurrently in parallel.
Parallel computing may be seen as a particular tightly coupled form of distributed computing, and distributed computing may be seen as a loosely coupled form of parallel computing.
Nevertheless, it is possible to roughly classify concurrent systems as "parallel" or "distributed" using the following criteria:
- In parallel computing, all processors may have access to a shared memory to exchange information between processors.
- In distributed computing, each processor has its own private memory (distributed memory).

Cluster computing

A cluster is a group of loosely coupled computers that work together closely, so that in some respects they can be regarded as a single computer. Clusters are composed of multiple standalone machines connected by a network. While machines in a cluster do not have to be symmetric, load balancing is more difficult if they are not. The most common type of cluster is the Beowulf cluster, which is a cluster implemented on multiple identical commercial off-the-shelf computers connected with a TCP/IP Ethernet local area network. Beowulf technology was originally developed by Thomas Sterling and Donald Becker. The vast majority of the TOP500 supercomputers are clusters.

Massive parallel processing

A massively parallel processor (MPP) is a single computer with many networked processors. MPPs have many of the same characteristics as clusters, but MPPs have specialized interconnect networks (whereas clusters use commodity hardware for networking). MPPs also tend to be larger than clusters, typically having "far more" than 100 processors.In a MPP, "each CPU contains its own memory and copy of the operating system and application.

Each subsystem communicates with the others via a high-speed interconnect."

Blue Gene/L, the fifth fastest supercomputer in the world according to the June 2009 TOP500 ranking, is a MPP.

Grid computing

Most grid computing applications use middleware, software that sits between the operating system and the application to manage network resources and standardize the software interface. The most common distributed computing middleware is the Berkeley Open Infrastructure for Network Computing (BOINC). Often, distributed computing software makes use of "spare cycles", performing computations at times when a computer is idling.

Specialized parallel computers

Within parallel computing, there are specialized parallel devices that remain niche areas of interest. While not domain-specific, they tend to be applicable to only a few classes of parallel problems.

Reconfigurable computing with field-programmable gate arrays

Reconfigurable computing is the use of a field-programmable gate array (FPGA) as a co-processor to a general-purpose computer. An FPGA is, in essence, a computer chip that can rewire itself for a given task.
FPGAs can be programmed with hardware description languages such as VHDL or Verilog. However, programming in these languages can be tedious. Several vendors have created C to HDL languages that attempt to emulate the syntax and semantics of the C programming language, with which most programmers are familiar. The best known C to HDL languages are Mitrion-C, Impulse C, DIME-C, and Handel-C. Specific subsets of SystemC based on C++ can also be used for this purpose.

AMD's decision to open its HyperTransport technology to third-party vendors has become the enabling technology for high-performance reconfigurable computing. According to Michael R. D'Amour, Chief Operating Officer of DRC Computer Corporation, "when we first walked into AMD, they called us 'the socket stealers. Now they call us their partners."

General-purpose computing on graphics processing units (GPGPU)

General-purpose computing on graphics processing units (GPGPU) is a fairly recent trend in computer engineering research. GPUs are co-processors that have been heavily optimized for computer graphics
processing.] Computer graphics processing is a field dominated by data parallel operations—particularly linear algebra matrix operations.
In the early days, GPGPU programs used the normal graphics APIs for executing programs. However, several new programming languages and platforms have been built to do general purpose computation on GPUs with both Nvidia and AMD releasing programming environments with CUDA and Stream SDK respectively. Other GPU programming languages include BrookGPU, PeakStream, and RapidMind. Nvidia has also released specific products for computation in their Tesla series. The technology consortium Khronos Group has released the OpenCL specification, which is a framework for writing programs that execute across platforms consisting of CPUs and GPUs. AMD, Apple, Intel, Nvidia and others are supporting OpenCL.

Application-specific integrated circuits

Several application-specific integrated circuit (ASIC) approaches have been devised for dealing with parallel applications.

Because an ASIC is (by definition) specific to a given application, it can be fully optimized for that application. As a result, for a given application, an ASIC tends to outperform a general-purpose computer. However, ASICs are created by X-ray lithography. This process requires a mask, which can be extremely expensive.

A single mask can cost over a million US dollars. (The smaller the transistors required for the chip, the more expensive the mask will be.) Meanwhile, performance increases in general-purpose computing over time (as described by Moore's Law) tend to wipe out these gains in only one or two chip generations. High initial cost, and the tendency to be overtaken by Moore's-law-driven general-purpose computing, has rendered ASICs unfeasible for most parallel computing applications. However, some have been built. One example is the peta-flop RIKEN MDGRAPE-3 machine which uses custom ASICs for molecular dynamics simulation.

Vector processors

A vector processor is a CPU or computer system that can execute the same instruction on large sets of data. "Vector processors have high-level operations that work on linear arrays of numbers or vectors. An example vector operation is A = B × C, where A, B, and C are each 64-element vectors of 64-bit floating-point numbers."[21] They are closely related to Flynn's SIMD classification.
Cray computers became famous for their vector-processing computers in the 1970s and 1980s. However, vector processors—both as CPUs and as full computer systems—have generally disappeared. Modern processor instruction sets do include some vector processing instructions, such as with AltiVec and Streaming SIMD Extensions (SSE).
The Cray-1 is the most famous vector processor.

PERFORMANCE EVALUATION

The primary attributes used to measure the performance of a computer system are as follows.

Cycle time(T): It is the unit of time for all the operations of a computer system. It is the inverse of clock rate (l/f). The cycle time is represented in n sec.

Cycles Per Instruction(CPI): Different instructions takes different number of cycles for execution. CPI is measurement of number of cycles per instruction

Instruction count(I_c): Number of instruction in a program is called instruction count. If we assume that all instructions have same number of cycles, then the total execution time of a program
= number of instruction in the program * number of cycle required by one instruction * time of one cycle.

Hence, execution time T=I_c*CPI*Tsec.

Practically the clock frequency of the system is specified in MHz. Also, the processor speed is measured in terms of million instructions per sec(MIPS).

The Concept of Concurrent and Parallel Execution

Real world systems are naturally concurrent, and computer science is about modeling the real world. Examples of real world systems which require concurrency are railway networks and machines in a factory. In the computer world, many new operating systems support concurrency. While working on our personal computers, we may download a file, listen to streaming audio, have a clock running , print something and type in a text editor. A multiprocessor or a distributed computer system can better exploit the inherent concurrency in problem solutions than a uniprocessor system. Concurrency is achieved either by creating simultaneous processes or by creating threads within a process. Whichever of these methods is used, it requires a lot of effort to synchronise the processes/threads to avoid race conditions, deadlocks and starvations.

Study of concurrent and parallel executions is important due to following reasons:

- Some problems are most naturally solved by using a set of co-operating processes.
- To reduce the execution time.

The words "concurrent" and "parallel" are often used interchangeably, however they are distinct.

Concurrent execution is the temporal behaviour of the N-client 1 -server model where only one client is served at any given moment. It has dual nature; it is sequential in a small time scale, but simultaneous in a large time scale. In our context, a processor works as server and process or thread works as client. Examples of concurrent languages include Adam, concurrent Pascal, Modula-2 and concurrent PROLOG).

Parallel execution is associated with the N-client N-server model. It allows the servicing of more than one client at the same time as the number of servers is more than one. Examples of parallel languages includes Occam-2, Parallel C and strand-88.

Parallel execution does not need explicit concurrency in the language. Parallelism can be achieved by the underlying hardware. Similarly, we can have concurrency in a language without parallel execution. This is the case when a program is executed on a single processor.

Granularity

Granularity refers to the amount of computation done in parallel relative to the size of the whole program. In parallel computing, granularity is a qualitative measure of the ratio of computation to communication. According to granularity of the system, parallel-processing systems can be divided into two groups: fine-grain systems and coarse-grain systems. In fine-grained systems, parallel parts are relatively small and that means more frequent communication. They have low computation to communication ratio and require high communication overhead. In coarse-grained systems parallel parts are relatively large and that means more computation and less communication. If granularity is too fine it is possible that the overhead required for communications and synchronization between tasks takes longer than the computation. On the other hand, in coarse-grain parallel systems, relatively large amount of computational work is done. They have high computation to communication ratio and imply more opportunity for performance increase.

The extent of granularity in a system is determined by the algorithm applied and the hardware environment in which it runs. On an architecturally neutral system, the granularity does affect the performance of the resulting program. The communication of data required to start a large process may take a considerable amount of time. On the other hand, a large process will often have less communication to do during processing.

A process may need only a small amount of data to get going, but may need to receive more data to continue processing, or may need to do a lot of communication with other processes in order to perform its processing. In most cases the overhead associated with communications and synchronization is high relative to execution speed so it is advantageous to have coarse granularity.

Potential of Parallelism

Problems in the real world vary in respect of the degree of inherent parallelism inherent in the respective problem domain. Some problems may be easily parallelized. On the other hand, there are some inherent sequential problems (for example computation of Fibonacci sequence) whose parallelization is nearly impossible. The extent of parallelism may be improved by appropriate design of an algorithm to solve the problem consideration. If processes don't share address space and we could eliminate data dependency among instructions, we can achieve higher level of parallelism. The concept of speed up is used as a measure of the *speed up* that indicates up to what extent to which a sequential program can be parallelized. Speed up may be taken as a sort of degree of inherent parallelism in a program.

In this respect, Amdahl, has given a law, known as Amdahl's Law, which states that potential program speedup is defined by the fraction of code (P) that can be parallelized:

$$\text{Speed up} = \frac{1}{1 - P}$$

If no part of the code can be parallelized, P = 0 and the speedup = 1 i.e. it is an inherently sequential program. If all of the code is parallelized, P = 1, the speedup is infinite. But practically, the code in no program can made 100% parallel. Hence speed up can never be infinite.

If 50% of the code can be parallelized, maximum speedup = 2, meaning the code will run twice as fast.

If we introduce the number of processors performing the parallel fraction of work, the relationship can be modeled by:

$$\text{Speed up} = \frac{1}{P/N + S}$$

Where P = parallel fraction, N = number of processors and S = serial fraction.

Table 1 Speedup

N	P = .50	P = .90	P = .99
10	1.82	5.26	9.17
100	1.98	9.17	50.25
1000	1.99	9.91	90.99
10000	1.99	9.91	99.02

The *Table 1* suggests that speed up increases as P increases. However, after a certain limits N does not have much impact on the value of speed up. The reason being that, for N processors to remain active, the code should be, in some way or other, be divisible in roughly N parts, independent part, each part taking almost same amount of time.

DATA CLUSTERING

Clustering is the task of dividing the population or data points into a number of groups such that data points in the same groups are more similar to other data points in the same group than those in other groups. In simple words, the aim is to segregate groups with similar traits and assign them into clusters.

Let's understand this with an example. Suppose, you are the head of a rental store and wish to understand preferences of your costumers to scale up your business. Is it possible for you to look at details of each costumer and devise a unique business strategy for each one of them? Definitely not. But, what you can do is to cluster all of your costumers into say 10 groups based on their purchasing habits and use a separate strategy for costumers in each of these 10 groups. And this is what we call clustering.

Now, that we understand what is clustering. Let's take a look at the types of clustering.

Types of Clustering

Broadly speaking, clustering can be divided into two subgroups :

• Hard Clustering: In hard clustering, each data point either belongs to a cluster completely or not. For example, in the above example each customer is put into one group out of the 10 groups.

• Soft Clustering: In soft clustering, instead of putting each data point into a separate cluster, a probability or likelihood of that data point to be in those clusters is assigned. For example, from the above scenario each costumer is assigned a probability to be in either of 10 clusters of the retail store.

MINSKY'S CONJECTURE

Minsky's conjecture states that due to the need for parallel processors to communicate with each other, speedup increases as the logarithm of the number of processing elements, see figure 8.2.3-1. This would make large-scale parallelism unproductive.

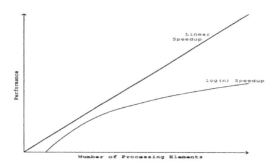

Figure: Minsky's Conjecture

Minsky's evidence for this comes from parallel computers of the late 60's and early 70's which had 2-4 processors. At this time communication was not very well catered for and Minsky's conjecture held. Two innovations have changed this state of affairs and today's parallel computers often achieve almost linear speedup. Clever multitasking allows processors to interleave processing with relatively low speed communications. Multitasking can dramatically reduce the amount of time wasted by a processor waiting around during communication.

The other development is to use 'Direct Memory Access' (DMA) like units to do the communication for the processor, the transputer does this with its link engines, see section 4.4. The DMA unit is told what to transmit, and where to transmit it, while the processor can get on with other tasks. By cycle stealing the DMA can further reduce the amount by which communication impinges on computation. In this way the processor has effectively been decoupled from communication.

It has been further argued that as the number of processors grows so does the amount of communications and at some point, even with high speed DMA communications, speedup will be limited, see figure 2. On a single processor a process makes data available to a second processes by saving it in memory from where the second process can read it. This is communication between processes, even though both processes reside on the same processor. If that piece of data needs to be made available to a process on another processor then it can just as easily be sent to an I/O unit than to a memory unit - the cost is comparable.

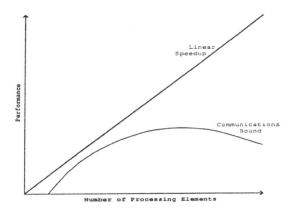

Figure: Crippling Communications Overhead

The main advantage of main memory as a communications medium is that all the data is made available to all the processes. On a message passing parallel computer if it is not known which data will be needed by a particular processor then problems can occur. Either all data has to be transmitted to all processors or the processor wishing to use the data must find out where it is and request it.

Fortunately, there are many applications where an almost linear data flow graph can be drawn between processes. In these cases data use is completely predictable and the algorithm can ensure that data is sent to where it is needed. In essence the point at which an application becomes communications bound is a product of both the number of processors the topology and the algorithm. For many applications the algorithm can be adjusted to maintain almost linear speedup. Sometimes Minsky's Conjecture is observed, however, this can regarded as a worst case scenario and usually changing the algorithm gives much better results.

THE NEED OF PARALLEL COMPUTATION

With the progress of computer science, computational speed of the processors has also increased many a time. However, there are certain constraints as we go upwards and face large complex problems. So we have to look for alternatives. The answer lies in parallel computing. There are two primary reasons for using parallel computing: save time and solve larger problems. It is obvious that with the increase in number of processors working in parallel, computation time is bound to reduce.

Also, they're some scientific problems that even the fastest processor to takes months or even years to solve. However, with the application of parallel computing these problems may be solved in a few hours. Other reasons to adopt parallel computing are:

Cost savings: We can use multiple cheap computing resources instead of paying heavily for a supercomputer.

Overcoming memory constraints: Single computers have very finite memory resources. For large problems, using the memories of multiple computers may overcome this obstacle. So if we combine the memory resources of multiple computers then we can easily fulfill the memory requirements of the large-size problems.

Limits to serial computing: Both physical and practical factors pose significant constraints to simply building ever faster serial computers. The speed of a serial computer is directly dependent upon how fast data can move through hardware. Absolute limits are the speed of light ($3*10^8$ m/sec) and the transmission limit of copper wire ($9*10^8$ m/sec). Increasing speeds necessitate increasing proximity of processing elements. Secondly, processor technology is allowing an increasing number of transistors to be placed on a chip. However, even with molecular or atomic -level components, a limit will be reached on how small components can be made. It is increasingly expensive to make a single processor faster. Using a larger number of moderately fast commodity processors to achieve the same (or better) performance is less expensive.

LEVELS OF PARALLEL PROCESSING

Depending upon the problem under consideration, parallelism in the solution of the problem may be achieved at different levels and in different ways. This section discusses various levels of parallelism. Parallelism in a problem and its possible solutions may be exploited either manually by the programmer or through automating compilers. We can have parallel processing at five levels.

Bit Level

From the advent of *very-large-scale integration* (VLSI) computer-chip fabrication technology in the 1970s until about 1986, speed-up in computer architecture was driven by doubling *computer word size*—the amount of information the processor can manipulate per cycle.[32] Increasing the word size reduces the number of instructions the processor must execute to perform an operation on variables whose sizes are greater than the length of the word.

For example, where an *8-bit* processor must add two *16-bit integers*, the processor must first add the 8 lower-order bits from each integer using the standard addition instruction, then add the 8 higher-order bits using an add-with-carry instruction and the *carry bit* from the lower order addition; thus, an 8-bit processor requires two instructions to complete a single operation, where a 16-bit processor would be able to complete the operation with a single instruction.

Historically, *4-bit* microprocessors were replaced with 8-bit, then 16-bit, then 32-bit microprocessors. This trend generally came to an end with the introduction of 32-bit processors, which has been a standard in general-purpose computing for two decades. Not until the early 2000s, with the advent of *x86-64* architectures, did *64-bit* processors become commonplace.

Instruction Level

It refers to the situation where different instructions of a program are executed by different processing elements. Most processors have several execution units and can execute several instructions (usually machine level) at the same time. Good compilers can reorder instructions to maximize instruction throughput. Often the processor itself can do this. Modern processors even parallelize execution of micro-steps of instructions within the same pipe. The earliest use of instruction level parallelism in designing PE's to enhance processing speed is pipelining. Pipelining was extensively used in early Reduced Instruction Set Computer (RISC). After RISC, super scalar processors were developed which execute multiple instruction in one clock cycle. The super scalar processor design exploits the parallelism available at instruction level by enhancing the number of arithmetic and functional units in PE's. The concept of instruction level parallelism was further modified and applied in the design of Very

Large Instruction Word (VLIW) processor, in which one instruction word encodes more than one operation. The idea of executing a number of instructions of a program in parallel by scheduling them on a single processor has been a major driving force in the design of recent processors

Loop Level

At this level, consecutive loop iterations are the candidates for parallel execution. However, data dependencies between subsequent iterations may restrict parallel execution of instructions at loop level. There is a lot of scope for parallel execution at loop level.

Example: In the following loop in C language,

$$for (i=0; i <= n; i++) A(i) = B(i)+ C(i)$$

Each of the instruction A(i) =B(i)+C(i) can be executed by different processing elements provided there are at least n processing elements. However, the instructions in the loop:

$$for (J=0, J<= n, J++) A(J) = A(J-1) + B(J)$$

cannot be executed parallelly as A(J) is data dependent on A(J-1) . This means that before exploiting the loop level parallelism the data dependencies must be checked:

Procedure Level

Here, parallelism is available in the form of parallel executable procedures. In this case, the design of the algorithm plays a major role. For example each thread in Java can be spawned to run a function or method.

Program Level

This is usually the responsibility of the operating system, which runs processes concurrently. Different programs are obviously independent of each other. So parallelism can be extracted by operating the system at this level.

APPLICATIONS OF PARALLEL COMPUTING

Parallel computing is an evolution of serial computing that attempts to emulate what has always been the state of affairs in the natural world. In the natural world, it is quite common to find many complex, interrelated events happening at the same time. Examples of concurrent processing in natural and man-made environments include:

Automobile assembly line
Daily operations within a business
Building a shopping mall
Ordering an aloo tikki burger at the drive through.
Hence, parallel computing has been considered to be "the high end of computing" and has been motivated by numerical simulations of complex systems and "Grand Challenge Problems" such as:

- Weather forecasting
- Predicting results of chemical and nuclear reactionsDNA structures of various species
- Design of mechanical devices
- Design of electronic circuits

- Design of complex manufacturing processes
- Accessing of large databases
- Design of oil exploration systems
- Design of web search engines, web based business services
- Design of computer-aided diagnosis in medicine
- Development of MIS for national and multi-national corporations
- Development of advanced graphics and virtual reality software, particularly for the entertainment industry, including networked video and multi-media technologies
- Collaborative work (virtual) environments

Scientific Applications/Image processing

Most of parallel processing applications from science and other academic disciplines, are mainly have based upon numerical simulations where vast quantities of data must be processed, in order to create or test a model. Examples of such applications include:

- Global atmospheric circulation,
- Blood flow circulation in the heart,
- The evolution of galaxies,
- Atomic particle movement,
- Optimisation of mechanical components.

The production of realistic moving images for television and the film industry has become a big business. In the area of large computer animation, though much of the work can be done on high specification workstations, yet the input will often involve the application of parallel processing. Even at the cheap end of the image production spectrum, affordable systems for small production companies have been formed by connecting cheap PC technology using a small LAN to farm off processing work on each image to be produced.

Engineering Applications

Some of the engineering applications are:
- Simulations of artificial ecosystems,
- Airflow circulation over aircraft components.

Airflow circulation is a particularly important application. A large aircraft design company might perform up to five or six full body simulations per working day.

Database Query/Answering Systems

There are a large number of opportunities for speed-up through parallelizing a Database Management System. However, the actual application of parallelism required depends very much on the application area that the

DBMS is used for. For example, in the financial sector the DBMS generally is used for short simple transactions, but with a high number of transactions per second. On the other hand in a Computer Aided Design (CAD) situation (e.g., VLSI design) the transactions would be long and with low traffic rates. In a Text query system, the database would undergo few updates, but would be required to do complex pattern matching queries over a large number of entries. An example of a computer designed to speed up database queries is the Teradata computer, which employs parallelism in processing complex queries.

AI Applications

Search is a vital component of an AI system, and the search operations are performed over large quantities of complex structured data using unstructured inputs. Applications of parallelism include:

- Search through the rules of a production system,
- Using fine-grain parallelism to search the semantic networks created by NETL,
- Implementation of Genetic Algorithms,
- Neural Network processors,
- Preprocessing inputs from complex environments, such as visual stimuli.

Mathematical Simulation and Modeling Applications

The tasks involving mathematical simulation and modeling require a lot of parallel processing. Three basic formalisms in mathematical simulation and modeling are Discrete Time System Simulation (DTSS), Differential Equation System Simulation (DESS) and Discrete Event System Simulation (DEVS). All other formalisms are combinations of these three formalisms. DEVS is the most popular. Consequently a number of software tools have been designed for DEVS. Some of such softwares are:

- Parsec, a C-based simulation language for sequential and parallel execution of discrete-event simulation models.
- Omnet++ a discrete-event simulation software development environment written in C++.
- Desmo-J a Discrete event simulation framework in Java.
- Adevs (A Discrete Event System simulator) is a C++ library for constructing discrete event simulations based on the Parallel DEVS and Dynamic Structure DEVS formalisms.

Any Logic is a professional simulation tool for complex discrete, continuous and hybrid systems.

FUTURE OF PARALLEL COMPUTERS

It has been relatively easy to arrive at the state where a single processor can accept several users and still appear to each user as though they are the only one using the machine. It has only recently become practical to invert this situation: where a single user is given simultaneous command of several processors. Consequently, the environments for this condition are still evolving.

The next logical stage - which has already started with machines like the Edinburgh Regional Supercomputer - is to build an environment where many users work on a computer with many processors. Although this is already possible, the way in which resources are allocated is still too crude to be considered a mature product. The management of resources, such as memory and backing store, are still in evolution for uniprocessors - though the rate has slowed down. The ability to treat computing power as a dynamic resource is a new and unfamiliar concept and much work still needs to be done.

Another possible way forward for parallel computers is to have processing elements distributed amongst many networked workstations. Each workstation would have 10-100 processing elements to speed up its local performance. When a workstation is not being used, a global operating system would enlist all its processing elements to form a pool of 'out workers'. The operating system could then distribute work from particularly busy workstations to all the out workers. This approach has been used with some success at the Inmos design laboratories at Bristol. Furthermore, as local networks rapidly increase the bandwidth of their links, distributed processing will make inroads into multiprocessing.

Software

The single greatest thing holding back parallel computers is lack of off-the-shelf applications software. This underlies that fact that the architectures of parallel computers are much more diverse than the architectures of serial computers.

Furthermore, there is a need for a standard parallel operating system, in a similar manner to the way Unix is a standard. A standard would allow many people to use the machine via a familiar environment. (Many manufacturers already use a superset of the UNIX operating system, but the supersets are not compatible with each other.)

It could be said that the main advantage of a standard operating environment is that it hides the details of a machine from the user. The users are treated to an abstract machine. On a parallel computer, the details (eg architecture, topology) can drastically effect the machine's performance on various programs. However, returning the details of the machine to the user is unpopular because there is more to learn.

Automatic dynamic load balancing and automatic message routing can only ever be partially effective. Knowledge of a machines topology and the likely loading, along with some static load balancing can give rise to improvements of several orders of magnitude.

Much work still has to be done in devising fundamental parallel algorithms. Many of these will initially be roughly hacked up serial algorithms, but in many cases there is scope for a totally new parallel approach. The relationship between computer topology and parallel algorithm is of fundamental importance in this field and has not yet been adequately addressed.

2

CLASSIFICATION OF PARALLEL COMPUTERS

Introduction
Types of Classification
Flynn's Classification
      Instruction Cycle
      Instruction Stream and Data Stream
      Flynn's Classification
Handler's Classification
Structural Classification
Shared Memory System/Tightly Coupled System
      Uniform Memory Access Model
      Non-Uniform Memory Access Model
      Cache-only Memory Architecture Model
Loosely Coupled Systems
 Classification Based on Grain Size
 Parallelism Conditions
 Bernstein Conditions for Detection of Parallelism
 Parallelism Based on Grain Size

INTRODUCTION

Parallel computers are those that emphasize the parallel processing between the operations in some way. In the previous unit, all the basic terms of parallel processing and computation have been defined. Parallel computers can be characterized based on the data and instruction streams forming various types of computer organisations. They can also be classified based on the computer structure, e.g. multiple processors having separate memory or one shared global memory. Parallel processing levels can also be defined based on the size of instructions in a program called grain size. Thus, parallel computers can be classified based on various criteria. This unit discusses all types of classification of parallel computers based on the above mentioned criteria.

TYPES OF CLASSIFICATION

The following classification of parallel computers have been identified:

- Classification based on the instruction and data streams
- Classification based on the structure of computers
- Classification based on how the memory is accessed
- Classification based on grain size

FLYNN'S CLASSIFICATION

This classification was first studied and proposed by Michael Flynn in 1972. Flynn did not consider the machine architecture for classification of parallel computers; he introduced the concept of *instruction* and *data* streams for categorizing of computers. All the computers classified by Flynn are not parallel computers, but to grasp the concept of parallel computers, it is necessary to understand all types of

Flynn's classification. Since, this classification is based on instruction and data streams, first we need to understand how the instruction cycle works.

Instruction Cycle

The instruction cycle consists of a sequence of steps needed for the execution of an instruction in a program. A typical instruction in a program is composed of two parts: Opcode and Operand. The Operand part specifies the data on which the specified operation is to be done. (See *Figure 1*). The Operand part is divided into two parts: addressing mode and the Operand. The addressing mode specifies the method of determining the addresses of the actual data on which the operation is to be performed and the operand part is used as an argument by the method in determining the actual address.

Figure 1: Opcode and Operand

The control unit of the CPU of the computer fetches instructions in the program, one at a time. The fetched Instruction is then decoded by the decoder which is a part of the control unit and the processor executes the decoded instructions. The result of execution is temporarily stored in Memory Buffer Register (MBR) (also called Memory Data Register). The normal execution steps are shown in *Figure 2*.

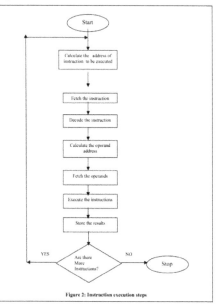

Figure 2: Instruction execution steps

28

Instruction Stream and Data Stream

The term 'stream' refers to a sequence or flow of either instructions or data operated on by the computer. In the complete cycle of instruction execution, a flow of instructions from main memory to the CPU is established. This flow of instructions is called **instruction stream.** Similarly, there is a flow of operands between processor and memory bi-directionally. This flow of operands is called **data stream.** These two types of streams are shown in *Figure 3*.

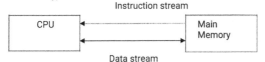

Figure 3: Instruction and data stream

Thus, it can be said that the sequence of instructions executed by CPU forms the Instruction streams and sequence of data (operands) required for execution of instructions form the Data streams.

Flynn's Classification

Flynn's classification is based on multiplicity of instruction streams and data streams observed by the CPU during program execution. Let I_s and D_s are minimum number of streams flowing at any point in the execution, then the computer organisation can be categorized as follows:

1) Single Instruction and Single Data stream (SISD)

In this organisation, sequential execution of instructions is performed by one CPU containing a single processing element (PE), i.e., ALU under one control unit as shown in *Figure 4*. Therefore, SISD machines are conventional serial computers that process only one stream of instructions and one stream of data. This type of computer organisation is depicted in the diagram:

$I_s = D_s = 1$

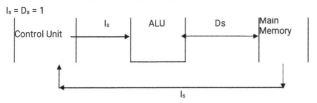

Figure 4: SISD Organisation

Examples of SISD machines include:

CDC 6600 which is unpipelined but has multiple functional units.
CDC 7600 which has a pipelined arithmetic unit.
Amdhal 470/6 which has pipelined instruction processing.
Cray-1 which supports vector processing.

2) Single Instruction and Multiple Data stream (SIMD)

In this organisation, multiple processing elements work under the control of a single control unit. It has one instruction and multiple data stream. All the processing elements of this organization receive the same instruction broadcast from the CU. Main memory can also be divided into modules for generating multiple data streams acting as a *distributed memory* as shown in *Figure 5*.

Therefore, all the processing elements simultaneously execute the same instruction and are said to be 'lock-stepped' together. Each processor takes the data from its own memory and hence it has on distinct data streams. (Some systems also provide a shared global memory for communications.) Every processor must be allowed to complete its instruction before the next instruction is taken for execution. Thus, the execution of instructions is synchronous. Examples of SIMD organisation are ILLIAC-IV, PEPE, BSP, STARAN, MPP, DAP and the Connection Machine (CM-1).

This type of computer organisation is denoted as:

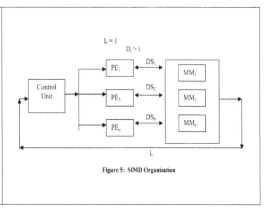

Figure 5: SIMD Organisation

3) Multiple Instruction and Single Data stream (MISD)

In this organization, multiple processing elements are organised under the control of multiple control units. Each control unit is handling one instruction stream and processed through its corresponding processing element. But each processing element is processing only a single data stream at a time. Therefore, for handling multiple instruction streams and single data stream, multiple control units and multiple processing elements are organised in this classification. All processing elements are interacting with the common shared memory for the organisation of single data stream as shown in *Figure 6*. The only known example of a computer capable of MISD operation is the C.mmp built by Carnegie-Mellon University.

This type of computer organisation is denoted as:

$I_s > 1 \ D_s = 1$

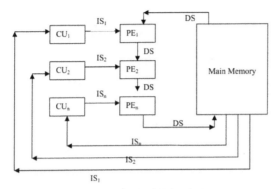

Figure 6: MISD Organisation

This classification is not popular in commercial machines as the concept of single data streams executing on multiple processors is rarely applied. But for the specialized applications, MISD organisation can be very helpful. For example, Real time computers need to be fault tolerant where several processors execute the same data for producing the redundant data.

This is also known as N- version programming. All these redundant data are compared as results which should be same; otherwise faulty unit is replaced. Thus MISD machines can be applied to fault tolerant real time computers.

4) Multiple Instruction and Multiple Data stream (MIMD)

In this organization, multiple processing elements and multiple control units are organized as in MISD. But the difference is that now in this organization multiple instruction streams operate on multiple data streams . Therefore, for handling multiple instruction streams, multiple control units and multiple processing elements are organized such that multiple processing elements are handling multiple data streams from the Main memory as shown in *Figure 7*. The processors work on their own data with their own instructions. Tasks executed by different processors can start or finish at different times. They are not lock-stepped, as in SIMD computers, but run asynchronously. This classification actually recognizes the parallel computer. That means in the real sense MIMD organisation is said to be a Parallel computer. All multiprocessor systems fall under this classification. Examples include; C.mmp, Burroughs D825, Cray-2, S1, Cray X- MP, HEP, Pluribus, IBM 370/168 MP, Univac 1100/80, Tandem/16, IBM 3081/3084, C.m*, BBN Butterfly, Meiko Computing Surface (CS-1), FPS T/40000, iPSC.

This type of computer organisation is denoted as:

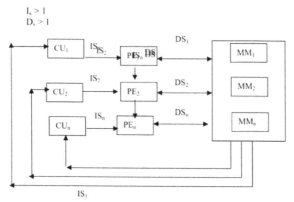

Of the classifications discussed above, MIMD organization is the most popular for a parallel computer. In the real sense, parallel computers execute the instructions in MIMD mode.

HANDLER'S CLASSIFICATION

In 1977, Wolfgang Handler proposed an elaborate notation for expressing the pipelining and parallelism of computers. Handler's classification addresses the computer at three distinct levels:

- Processor control unit (PCU),
- Arithmetic logic unit (ALU),
- Bit-level circuit (BLC).

The PCU corresponds to a processor or CPU, the ALU corresponds to a functional unit or a processing element and the BLC corresponds to the logic circuit needed to perform one-bit operations in the ALU.

Handler's classification uses the following three pairs of integers to describe a computer:

Computer = (p * p', a * a', b * b')

> Where p = number of PCUs
> Where p'= number of PCUs that can be pipelined Where a = number of ALUs controlled by each PCU Where a'= number of ALUs that can be pipelined
> Where b = number of bits in ALU or processing element (PE) word Where b'= number of pipeline segments on all ALUs or in a single PE

The following rules and operators are used to show the relationship between various elements of the computer:

The '*' operator is used to indicate that the units are pipelined or macro-pipelined with a stream of data running through all the units.

The '+' operator is used to indicate that the units are not pipelined but work on independent streams of data.

The 'v' operator is used to indicate that the computer hardware can work in one of several modes.

The '~' symbol is used to indicate a range of values for any one of the parameters.

Peripheral processors are shown before the main processor using another three pairs of integers. If the value of the second element of any pair is 1, it may omitted for brevity.

Handler's classification is best explained by showing how the rules and operators are used to classify several machines.

The CDC 6600 has a single main processor supported by 10 I/O processors. One control unit coordinates one ALU with a 60- bit word length. The ALU has 10 functional units which can be formed into a pipeline. The 10 peripheral I/O processors may work in parallel with each other and with the CPU. Each I/O processor contains one 12-bit ALU. The description for the 10 I/O processors is:

CDC 6600I/O = (10, 1, 12)

The description for the main processor is:

CDC 6600main = (1, 1 * 10, 60)

The main processor and the I/O processors can be regarded as forming a macro-pipeline so the '*' operator is used to combine the two structures:

CDC 6600 = (I/O processors) * (central processor = (10, 1, 12) * (1, 1 * 10, 60)

Texas Instrument's Advanced Scientific Computer (ASC) has one controller coordinating four arithmetic units. Each arithmetic unit is an eight stage pipeline with 64-bit words. Thus we have:

ASC = (1, 4, 64 * 8)

The Cray-1 is a 64 -bit single processor computer whose ALU has twelve functional units, eight of which can be chained together to from a pipeline. Different functional units have from 1 to 14 segments, which can also be pipelined. Handler's description of the Cray-1 is:

Cray-1 = (1, 12 * 8, 64 * (1 ~ 14))

Another sample system is Carnegie-Mellon University's C.mmp multiprocessor. This system was designed to facilitate research into parallel computer architectures and consequently can be extensively reconfigured. The system consists of 16 PDP-11 'minicomputers' (which have a 16-bit word length), interconnected by a crossbar switching network. Normally, the C.mmp operates in MIMD mode for which the description is (16, 1, 16). It can also operate in SIMD mode, where all the processors are coordinated by a single master controller. The SIMD mode description is (1, 16, 16). Finally, the system can be rearranged to operate in MISD mode. Here the processors are arranged in a chain with a single stream of data passing through all of them. The MISD modes description is (1 * 16, 1, 16). The 'v' operator is used to combine descriptions of the same piece of hardware operating in differing modes. Thus, Handler's description for the complete C.mmp is:

C.mmp = (16, 1, 16) v (1, 16, 16) v (1 * 16, 1, 16)

The '*' and '+' operators are used to combine several separate pieces of hardware. The 'v' operator is of a different form to the other two in that it is used to combine the different operating modes of a single piece of hardware.

While Flynn's classification is easy to use, Handler's classification is cumbersome. The direct use of numbers in the nomenclature of Handler's classification's makes it much more abstract and hence difficult. Handler's classification is highly geared towards the description of pipelines and chains. While it is well able to describe the parallelism in a single processor, the variety of parallelism in multiprocessor computers is not addressed well.

STRUCTURAL CLASSIFICATION

Flynn's classification discusses the behavioural concept and does not take into consideration the computer's structure. Parallel computers can be classified based on their structure also, which is discussed below and shown in *Figure 8*.

As we have seen, a parallel computer (MIMD) can be characterised as a set of multiple processors and shared memory or memory modules communicating via an interconnection network. When multiprocessors communicate through the global shared memory modules then this organisation is called **Shared memory computer** or **Tightly coupled systems** as shown in *Figure 9*. Similarly when every processor in a multiprocessor system, has its own local memory and the processors communicate via messages transmitted between their local memories, then this organisation is called **Distributed memory computer** or **Loosely coupled system** as shown in *Figure 10*. *Figures 9* and *10* show the simplified diagrams of both organisations.

The processors and memory in both organisations are interconnected via an interconnection network. This interconnection network may be in different forms like crossbar switch, multistage network, etc. which will be discussed in the next unit.

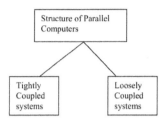

Figure 8: Structural classification

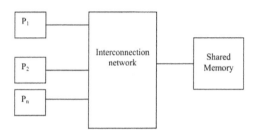

Figure 9: Tightly coupled system

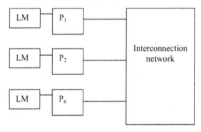

Figure 10 Loosely coupled system

Shared Memory System / Tightly Coupled System

Shared memory multiprocessors have the following characteristics:
Every processor communicates through a shared global memory.
For high speed real time processing, these systems are preferable as their throughput is high as
compared to loosely coupled systems.

In tightly coupled system organization, multiple processors share a global main memory, which may have many modules as shown in detailed *Figure 11*. The processors have also access to I/O devices. The inter- communication between processors, memory, and other devices are implemented through various interconnection networks, which are discussed below.

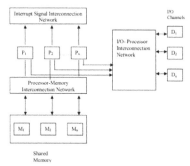

Figure 11: Tightly coupled system organization

Processor-Memory Interconnection Network (PMIN)

This is a switch that connects various processors to different memory modules. Connecting every processor to every memory module in a single stage while the crossbar switch may become complex. Therefore, multistage network can be adopted. There can be a conflict among processors such that they attempt to access the same memory modules. This conflict is also resolved by PMIN.

Input-Output-Processor Interconnection Network (IOPIN)

This interconnection network is used for communication between processors and I/O channels. All processors communicate with an I/O channel to interact with an I/O device with the prior permission of IOPIN.

Interrupt Signal Interconnection Network (ISIN)

When a processor wants to send an interruption to another processor, then this interrupt first goes to ISIN, through which it is passed to the destination processor. In this way, synchronisation between processor is implemented by ISIN. Moreover, in case of failure of one processor, ISIN can broadcast the message to other processors about its failure.

Since, every reference to the memory in tightly coupled systems is via interconnection network, there is a delay in executing the instructions. To reduce this delay, every processor may use cache memory for the frequent references made by the processor as shown in *Figure 12*.

The shared memory multiprocessor systems can further be divided into three modes which are based on the manner in which shared memory is accessed. These modes are shown in *Figure 13* and are discussed below.

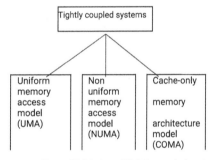

Figure 13: Modes of Tightly coupled systems

Uniform Memory Access Model (UMA)

In this model, main memory is uniformly shared by all processors in multiprocessor systems and each processor has equal access time to shared memory. This model is used for time-sharing applications in a multi user environment.

Non-Uniform Memory Access Model (NUMA)

In shared memory multiprocessor systems, local memories can be connected with every processor. The collection of all local memories form the global memory being shared. In this way, global memory is distributed to all the processors. In this case, the access to a local memory is uniform for its corresponding processor as it is attached to the local memory. But if one reference is to the local memory of some other remote processor, then the access is not uniform. It depends on the location of the memory. Thus, all memory words are not accessed uniformly.

Cache-Only Memory Access Model (COMA)

As we have discussed earlier, shared memory multiprocessor systems may use cache memories with every processor for reducing the execution time of an instruction. Thus in NUMA model, if we use cache memories instead of local memories, then it becomes COMA model. The collection of cache memories form a global memory space. The remote cache access is also non-uniform in this model.

Loosely Coupled Systems

These systems do not share the global memory because shared memory concept gives rise to the problem of memory conflicts, which in turn slows down the execution of instructions. Therefore, to alleviate this problem, each processor in loosely coupled systems is having a large local memory (LM), which is not shared by any other processor. Thus, such systems have multiple processors with their own local memory and a set of I/O devices. This set of processor, memory and I/O devices makes a computer system. Therefore, these systems are also called multi-computer systems. These computer systems are connected together via message passing interconnection network through which processes communicate by passing messages to one another. Since every computer system or node in multicomputer systems has a separate memory, they are called distributed multicomputer systems. These are also called loosely coupled systems, meaning that nodes have little coupling between them as shown in *Figure 14*.

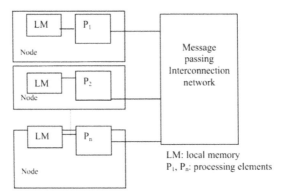

Figure 14: Loosely coupled system organisation

Since local memories are accessible to the attached processor only, no processor can access remote memory. Therefore, these systems are also known as no-remote memory access (NORMA) systems. Message passing interconnection network provides connection to every node and inter-node communication with message depends on the type of interconnection network. For example, interconnection network for a non-hierarchical system can be shared bus.

38

CLASSIFICATION BASED ON GRAIN SIZE

This classification is based on recognizing the parallelism in a program to be executed on a multiprocessor system. The idea is to identify the sub-tasks or instructions in a program that can be executed in parallel. For example, there are 3 statements in a program and statements S1 and S2 can be exchanged. That means, these are not sequential as shown in *Figure 15*. Then S1 and S2 can be executed in parallel.

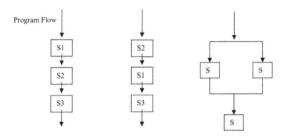

Figure 15: Parallel execution for S1 and S2

But it is not sufficient to check for the parallelism between statements or processes in a program. The decision of parallelism also depends on the following factors:
- Number and types of processors available, i.e., architectural features of host computer
- Memory organisation
- Dependency of data, control and resources

Parallelism Conditions

As discussed above, parallel computing requires that the segments to be executed in parallel must be independent of each other. So, before executing parallelism, all the conditions of parallelism between the segments must be analyzed. In this section, we discuss three types of dependency conditions between the segments (shown in *Figure 16*).

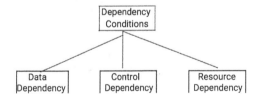

Figure 16: Dependency relations among the segments for parallelism

Data Dependency: It refers to the situation in which two or more instructions share same data. The instructions in a program can be arranged based on the relationship of data dependency; this means how two instructions or segments are data dependent on each other. The following types of data dependencies are recognised:

Flow Dependence : If instruction I_2 follows I_1 and output of I_1 becomes input of I_2, then I_2 is said to be flow dependent on I_1.
Antidependence : When instruction I_2 follows I_1 such that output of I_2 overlaps with the input of I_1 on the same data.
Output dependence : When output of the two instructions I_1 and I_2 overlap on the same data, the instructions are said to be output dependent.
I/O dependence : When read and write operations by two instructions are invoked on the same file, it is a situation of I/O dependence.

Consider the following program instructions:

I_1: a = b
I_2: c = a + d I_3: a = c

In this program segment instructions I_1 and I_2 are Flow dependent because variable a is generated by I_1 as output and used by I_2 as input. Instructions I_2 and I_3 are Antidependent because variable a is generated by I_3 but used by I_2 and in sequence I_2 comes first. I_3 is flow dependent on I_2 because of variable c. Instructions I_3 and I_1 are Output dependent because variable a is generated by both instructions.

Control Dependence: Instructions or segments in a program may contain control structures. Therefore, dependency among the statements can be in control structures also. But the order of execution in control structures is not known before the run time. Thus, control structures dependency among the instructions must be analyzed carefully. For example, the successive iterations in the following control structure are dependent on one another.

```
For ( i= 1; I<= n ; i++)
{
        if (x[i - 1] == 0) x[i] =0
        else
                x[i] = 1;
}
```

Resource Dependence : The parallelism between the instructions may also be affected due to the shared resources. If two instructions are using the same shared resource then it is a resource dependency condition. For example, floating point units or registers are shared, and this is known as *ALU dependency*. When memory is being shared, then it is called S*torage dependency.*

Bernstein Conditions for Detection of Parallelism

For execution of instructions or block of instructions in parallel, it should be ensured that the instructions are independent of each other. These instructions can be data dependent / control dependent / resource dependent on each other. Here we consider only data dependency among the statements for taking decisions of parallel execution. **A.J. Bernstein** has elaborated the work of data dependency and derived some conditions based on which we can decide the parallelism of instructions or processes.

Bernstein conditions are based on the following two sets of variables:
The Read set or input set R_I that consists of memory locations read by the statement of instruction I_1.
The Write set or output set W_I that consists of memory locations written into by instruction I_1.
The sets R_I and W_I are not disjoint as the same locations are used for reading and writing by S_I.

The following are Bernstein Parallelism conditions which are used to determine whether statements are parallel or not:

Locations in R_1 from which S_1 reads and the locations W_2 onto which S_2 writes must be mutually exclusive. That means S_1 does not read from any memory location onto which S_2 writes. It can be denoted as:

$R_1 \cap W_2 = \varphi$

Similarly, locations in R_2 from which S_2 reads and the locations W_1 onto which S_1 writes must be mutually exclusive. That means S_2 does not read from any memory location onto which S_1 writes. It can be denoted as: $R_2 \cap W_1 = \varphi$

The memory locations W_1 and W_2 onto which S_1 and S_2 write, should not be read by S_1 and S_2. That means R_1 and R_2 should be independent of W_1 and W_2. It can be denoted as : $W_1 \cap W_2 = \varphi$

To show the operation of Bernstein's conditions, consider the following instructions of sequential program:

$$I1 : x = (a + b) / (a * b)$$
$$I2 : y = (b + c) * d \quad I3 : z = x^2 + (a * e)$$

Now, the read set and write set of I1, I2 and I3 are as follows:

$$R_1 = \{a, b\} \qquad W_1 = \{x\}$$
$$R_2 = \{b, c, d\} \qquad W_2 = \{y\}$$
$$R_3 = \{x, a, e\} \qquad W_3 = \{z\}$$

Now let us find out whether I_1 and I_2 are parallel or not

$$R_1 \cap W_2 = \varphi$$
$$R_2 \cap W_1 = \varphi$$
$$W_1 \cap W_2 = \varphi$$

That means I_1 and I_2 are independent of each other.

Similarly for $I_1 \parallel I_3$,

$$R_1 \cap W_3 = \varphi$$
$$R_3 \cap W_1 \neq \varphi$$
$$W_1 \cap W_3 = \varphi$$

Hence I_1 and I_3 are not independent of each other.

For $I_2 \parallel I_3$,

$$R_2 \cap W_3 = \varphi$$
$$R_3 \cap W_2 = \varphi$$
$$W_3 \cap W_2 = \varphi$$

Hence, I_2 and I_3 are independent of each other.

Thus, I_1 and I_2, I_2 and I_3 are parallelizable but I_1 and I_3 are not.

Parallelism based on Grain size

Grain size: Grain size or Granularity is a measure which determines how much computation is involved in a process. Grain size is determined by counting the number of instructions in a program segment. The following types of grain sizes have been identified (shown in *Figure 17*):

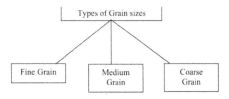

Figure 17: Types of Grain sizes

Fine Grain: This type contains approximately less than 20 instructions.
Medium Grain: This type contains approximately less than 500 instructions.
Coarse Grain: This type contains approximately greater than or equal to one thousand instructions.

Based on these grain sizes, parallelism can be classified at various levels in a program. These parallelism levels form a hierarchy according to which, lower the level, the finer is the granularity of the process. The degree of parallelism decreases with increase in level. Every level according to a grain size demands communication and scheduling overhead. Following are the parallelism levels (shown in *Figure 18*):

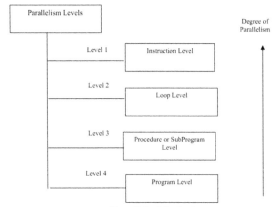

Figure 18: Parallelism Levels

Instruction level: This is the lowest level and the degree of parallelism is highest at this level. The fine grain size is used at instruction or statement level as only few instructions form the grain size here. The fine grain size may vary according to the type of the program. For example, for scientific applications, the instruction level grain size may be higher. As the higher degree of parallelism can be achieved at this level, the overhead for a programmer will be more.

Loop Level : This is another level of parallelism where iterative loop instructions can be parallelized. Fine grain size is used at this level also. Simple loops in a program are easy to parallelize whereas the recursive loops are difficult. This type of parallelism can be achieved through the compilers.

Procedure or SubProgram Level: This level consists of procedures, subroutines or subprograms. Medium grain size is used at this level containing some thousands of instructions in a procedure.

42

Multiprogramming is implemented at this level. Parallelism at this level has been exploited by programmers but not through compilers. Parallelism through compilers has not been achieved at the medium and coarse grain size.

Program Level: It is the last level consisting of independent programs for parallelism. Coarse grain size is used at this level containing tens of thousands of instructions. Time sharing is achieved at this level of parallelism. Parallelism at this level has been exploited through the operating system.

The relation between grain sizes and parallelism levels has been shown in *Table 1*.

Table 1: Relation between grain sizes and parallelism

Grain Size	Parallelism Level
Fine Grain	Instruction or Loop Level
Medium Grain	Procedure or SubProgram Level
Coarse Grain	Program Level

Coarse grain parallelism is traditionally implemented in tightly coupled or shared memory multiprocessors like the Cray Y-MP. Loosely coupled systems are used to execute medium grain program segments. Fine grain parallelism has been observed in SIMD organization of computers.

3

INTERCONNECTION NETWORK

Introduction
Network Properties
Design issues of Interconnection Network
Various Interconnection Networks
    Tree, Diamond Network, Mesh, Linear Array, Ring, Star, Hypercube, Chordal ring, Cube-connected-cycles, Perfect shuffle network, ILLIAC IV, Torus, Butterfly, Mesh-of-tree, Pyramid, Generalized Hyperbus, Twisted Cube Folded Hypercube, Incomplete Hypercube, Enhanced Incomplete Hypercube, Cross-Connected Cube, Banayan Hypercube.
Concept of Permutation Network
Performance Metrics

INTRODUCTION

This unit discusses the properties and types of interconnection networks. In multiprocessor systems, there are multiple processing elements, multiple I/O modules, and multiple memory modules. Each processor can access any of the memory modules and any of the I/O units. The connectivity between these is performed by interconnection networks.

Networking strategy was originally employed in the 1950's by the telephone industry as a means of reducing the time required for a call to go through. Similarly, the computer industry employs networking strategy to provide fast communication between computer subparts, particularly with regard to parallel machines.

The performance requirements of many applications, such as weather prediction, signal processing, radar tracking, and image processing, far exceed the capabilities of single-processor architectures. Parallel machines break a single problem down into parallel tasks that are performed concurrently, reducing significantly the application processing time.

Any parallel system that employs more than one processor per application program must be designed to allow its processors to communicate efficiently; otherwise, the advantages of parallel processing may be negated by inefficient communication. This fact emphasizes the importance of interconnection networks to overall parallel system performance. In many proposed or existing parallel processing architectures, an interconnection network is used to realize transportation of data between processors or between processors and memory modules.

This chapter deals with several aspects of the networks used in modern (and theoretical) computers. After classifying various network structures, some of the most well known networks are discussed, along with a list of advantages and disadvantages associated with their use. Some of the elements of network design are also explored to give the reader an understanding of the complexity of such designs.

Thus, an interconnection network is used for exchanging data between two processors in a multistage network. Memory bottleneck is a basic shortcoming of Von Newman architecture. In case of multiprocessor systems, the performance will be severely affected in case the data exchange between processors is delayed. The multiprocessor system has one global shared memory and each processor has a small local memory.

The processors can access data from memory associated with another processor or from shared memory using an interconnection network. Thus, interconnection networks play a central role in determining the overall performance of the multiprocessor systems. The interconnection networks are like customary network systems consisting of nodes and edges.

The nodes are switches having few input and few output (say n input and m output) lines. Depending upon the switch connection, the data is forwarded from input lines to output lines. The interconnection network is placed between various devices in the multiprocessor network.

The architecture of a general multiprocessor is shown in *Figure 1*. In the multiprocessor systems, these are multiple processor modules (each processor module consists of a processing element, small sized local memory and cache memory), shared global memory and shared peripheral devices.

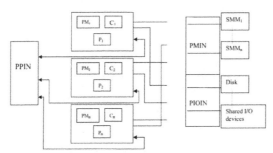

Figure 1: General Multi-Processor

PMIN = Processor to Memory Interconnection Network
PIOIN= Processor to I/O Interconnection Network
PPIN = Processor to Processor Interconnection Network
PM = Processor Module

Module communicates with other modules shared memory and peripheral devices using interconnection networks.

NETWORK PROPERTIES

The following properties are associated with interconnection networks.

Topology: It indicates how the nodes a network are organised.

Network Diameter. It is the minimum distance between the farthest nodes in a network. The distance is measured in terms of number of distinct hops between any two nodes.

Node degree: Number of edges connected with a node is called node degree. If the edge carries data from the node, it is called out degree and if this carries data into the node it is called in degree.

Bisection Bandwidth: Number of edges required to be cut to divide a network into two halves is called bisection bandwidth.

Latency: It is the delay in transferring the message between two nodes.

Network throughput: It is an indicative measure of the message carrying capacity of a network. It is defined as the total number of messages the network can transfer per unit time. To estimate the throughput, the capacity of the network and the messages number of actually carried by the network are calculated. Practically the throughput is only a fraction of its capacity.

In interconnection network the traffic flow between nodes may be nonuniform and it may be possible that a certain pair of nodes handles a disproportionately large amount of traffic. These are called "hot spot." The hot spot can behave as a bottleneck and can degrade the performance of the entire network.

Data Routing Functions: The data routing functions are the functions which when executed established the path between the source and the destination. In dynamic interconnection networks there can be various interconnection patterns that can be generated from a single network. This is done by executing various data routing functions. Thus data routing operations are used for routing the data between various processors. The data routing network can be static or dynamic static network

Hardware Cost: It refers to the cost involved in the implementation of an interconnection network. It includes the cost of switches, arbiter unit, connectors, arbitration unit, and interface logic.

Blocking and Non-Blocking network: In non-blocking networks the route from any free input node to any free output node can always be provided. Crossbar is an example of non-blocking network. In a blocking network simultaneous route establishment between a pair of nodes may not be possible. There may be situations where blocking can occur. Blocking refers to the situation where one switch is required to establish more than one connection simultaneously and end-to-end path cannot be established even if the input nodes and output nodes are free. The example of this is a blocking multistage network.

Static and Dynamic Interconnection Network: In a static network the connection between input and output nodes is fixed and cannot be changed. Static interconnection network cannot be reconfigured. The examples of this type of network are linear array, ring, chordal ring, tree, star, fat tree, mesh, tours, systolic arrays, and hypercube. This type of interconnection networks are more suitable for building computers where the communication pattern is more or less fixed, and can be implemented with static connections. In dynamic network the interconnection pattern between inputs and outputs can be changed. The interconnection pattern can be reconfigured according to the program demands. Here, instead of fixed connections, the switches or arbiters are used. Examples of such networks are buses, crossbar switches, and multistage networks. The dynamic networks are normally used in shared memory(SM) multiprocessors.

Dimensionality of Interconnection Network: Dimensionality indicates the Arrangement of nodes or processing elements in an interconnection network. In single dimensional or linear network, nodes are connected in a linear fashion; in two dimensional network the processing elements (PE's) are arranged in a grid and in cube network they are arranged in a three dimensional network.

Broadcast and Multicast: In the broadcast interconnection network, at one time one node transmits the data

and all other nodes receive that data. Broadcast is one to all mapping. It is the implementation achieved by SIMD computer systems. Message passing multi-computers also have broadcast networks. In multicast network manynodes are simultaneously allowed to transmit the data and multiple nodes receive the data.

DESIGN ISSUES OF INTERCONNECTION NETWORK

The following are the issues, which should be considered while designing an interconnection network.

Dimension and size of network: It should be decided how many PE's are there in the network and what the dimensionality of the network is i.e. with how many neighbours, each processor is connected.

Symmetry of the network: It is important to consider whether the network is symmetric or not i.e., whether all processors are connected with same number of processing elements, or the processing elements of corners or edges have different number of adjacent elements.

What is data communication strategy? Whether all processors are communicating with each other in one time unit synchronously or asynchronously on demand basis.

Message Size: What is message size? How much data a processor can send in one time unit.

Start up time: What is the time required to initiate the communication process.

Data transfer time: How long does it take for a message to reach to another processor. Whether this time is a function of link distance between two processors or it depends upon the number of nodes coming in between.

The interconnection network is static or dynamic: That means whether the configuration of interconnection network is governed by algorithm or the algorithm allows flexibility in choosing the path.

Various Interconnection Networks- NETWORK TOPOLOGY

Network topology refers to the layouts of links and switch boxes that establish interconnections. The links are essentially physical wires (or channels); the switch boxes are devices that connect a set of input links to a set of output links. There are two groups of network topologies: *static* and *dynamic*. Static networks provide fixed connections between nodes. (A node can be a processing unit, a memory module, an I/O module, or any combination thereof.) With a static network, links between nodes are unchangeable and cannot be easily reconfigured. Dynamic networks provide reconfigurable connections between nodes. The switch box is the basic component of the dynamic network. With a dynamic network the connections between nodes are established by the setting of a set of interconnected switch boxes.

In the following sections, examples of static and dynamic networks are discussed in detail.

Static Networks

There are various types of static networks, all of which are characterized by their node degree; node degree is the number of links (edges) connected to the node. Some well-known static networks are the following:

Degree 1:	*shared bus*
Degree 2:	*linear array, ring*
Degree 3:	*binary tree, fat tree, shuffle-exchange*
Degree 4:	*two-dimensional mesh (Illiac, torus)*
Varying degree:	*n-cube, n-dimensional mesh, k-ary n-cube*

A measurement unit, called *diameter*, can be used to compare the relative performance characteristics of different networks. More specifically, the diameter of a network is defined as the largest minimum distance between any pair of nodes. The minimum distance between a pair of nodes is the minimum number of communication links (hops) that data from one of the nodes must traverse in order to reach the other node.

In the following sections, the listed static networks are discussed in detail.

Shared bus. The shared bus, also called *common bus*, is the simplest type of static network. The shared bus has a degree of 1. In a shared bus architecture, all the nodes share a common communication link, as shown in Figure 2. The shared bus is the least expensive network to implement. Also, nodes (units) can be easily added or deleted from this network. However, it requires a mechanism for handling conflict when several nodes request the bus simultaneously. This mechanism can be achieved through a bus controller, which gives access to the bus either on a first-come, first-served basis or through a priority scheme. The shared bus has a diameter of 1 since each node can access the other nodes through the shared bus.

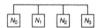

Figure 2: Shared bus.

Linear array. The linear array (degree of 2) has each node connected with two neighbors (except the far-ends nodes). The linear quality of this structure comes from the fact that the first and last nodes are not connected, as illustrated in Figure 3. Although the linear array has a simple structure, its design can mean long communication delays, especially between far-end nodes. This is because any data entering the network from one end must pass through a number of nodes in order to reach the other end of the network. A linear array, with N nodes, has a diameter of N-1.

Figure 3: Linear array.

Ring. Another networking configuration with a simple design is the ring structure. A ring network has a degree of 2. Similar to the linear array, each node is connected to two of its neighbors, but in this case the first and last nodes are also connected to form a ring. Figure 4 shows a ring network. A ring can be unidirectional or bidirectional. In a unidirectional ring the data can travel in only one direction, clockwise or counterclockwise. Such a ring has a diameter of N-1, like the linear array. However, a bidirectional ring, in which data travel in both directions, reduces the diameter by a factor of 2, or less if N is even. A bidirectional ring network's reliability, as compared to the linear array, is also improved. If a node should fail, effectively cutting off the connection in one direction, the other direction can be used to complete a message transmission. Once the connection is lost between any two adjacent nodes, the ring becomes a linear array, however.

Figure 4: Ring.

Cross Bar: The crossbar network is the simplest interconnection network. It has a two dimensional grid of switches. It is a non-blocking network and provides connectivity between inputs and outputs and it is possible to join any of the inputs to any output.

An N * M crossbar network is shown in the following *Figure 5 (a)* and switch connections are shown in *Figure 5 (b)*.

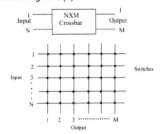

A switch positioned at a cross point of a particular row and particular column. connects that particular row (input) to column (output).

The hardware cost of N*N crossbar switch is proportional to N^2. It creates delay equivalent to one switching operation and the routing control mechanism is easy. The crossbar network requires N^2 switches for N input and N output network.

Binary tree. Figure 6 represents the structure of a binary tree with seven nodes. The top node is called the root, the four nodes at the bottom are called leaf (or terminal) nodes, and the rest of the nodes are called intermediate nodes. In such a network, each intermediate node has two children. The root has node address 1. The addresses of the children of a node are obtained by appending 0 and 1 to the node's address that is, the children of node *x* are labeled 2*x* and 2*x*+1. A binary tree with *N* nodes has diameter 2(*h*-1), where *h* is the height of the tree. The binary tree has the advantages of being expandable and having a simple implementation. Nonetheless, it can still cause long communication delays between faraway leaf nodes. Leaf nodes farthest away from each other must ultimately pass their message through the root. Since traffic increases as the root is approached, leaf nodes farthest away from each other will spend the most amount of time waiting for a message to traverse the tree from source to destination.

One desirable characteristic for an interconnection network is that data can be routed between the nodes in a simple manner (remember, a node may represent a processor). The binary tree has a simple routing algorithm. Let a packet denote a unit of information that a node needs to send to another node. Each packet has a header that contains routing information, such as source address and destination address. A packet is routed upward toward the root node until it reaches a node that is either the destination or ancestor of the destination node. If the current node is an ancestor of the destination node, the packet is routed downward toward the destination.

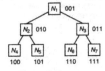

Figure 6 Binary tree.

Fat tree. One problem with the binary tree is that there can be heavy traffic toward the root node. Consider that the root node acts as the single connection point between the left and right subtrees. As can be observed in Figure 5, all messages from nodes N_2, N_4, and N_5 to nodes N_3, N_6, and N_7 have no choice but to pass through the root. To reduce the effect of such a problem, the fat tree was proposed by Leiserson. Fat trees are more like real trees in which the branches get thicker near the trunk. Proceeding up from the leaf nodes of a fat tree to the root, the number of communication links increases, and therefore the communication bandwidth increases. The communication bandwidth of an interconnection network is the expected number of requests that can be accepted per unit of time.

The structure of the fat tree is based on a binary tree. Each edge of the binary tree corresponds to two channels of the fat tree. One of the channels is from parent to child, and the other is from child to parent. The number of communication links in each channel increases as we go up the tree from the leaves and is determined by the amount of hardware available. For example, Figure 7 represents a fat tree in which the number of communication links in each channel is increased by 1 from one level of the tree to the next. The fat tree can be used to interconnect the processors of a general-purpose parallel machine. Since its communication bandwidth can be scaled independently from the number of processors, it provides great flexibility in design.

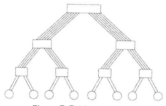

Figure 7: Fat tree.

Ring: This is a simple linear array where the end nodes are connected. It is equivalent to a mesh with wrap around connections. The data transfer in a ring is normally one direction. Thus, one drawback to this network is that some data transfer may require N/2 links to be traveled (like nodes 2 & 1) where N is the total number of nodes.

Shuffle-exchange. Another method for establishing networks is the shuffle-exchange connection. The shuffle-exchange network is a combination of two functions: *shuffle* and *exchange*. Each is a simple bijection function in which each input is mapped onto one and only one output. Let $S_{n-1} S_{n-2} \ldots S_0$ be the binary representation of a node address; then the shuffle function can be described as

$$\text{shuffle}(S_{n-1} S_{n-2} \ldots S_0) = S_{n-2} S_{n-3} \ldots S_0 S_{n-1}.$$

The reason that the function is called shuffle is that it reflects the process of shuffling cards. Given that there are eight cards, the shuffle function performs a perfect playing card shuffle as follows. First, the deck is cut in half, between cards 3 and 4.

Then the two half decks are merged by selecting cards from each half in an alternative order. Figure 9 represents how the cards are shuffled.

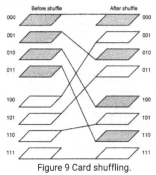

Figure 9 Card shuffling.

Another way to define shuffle connection is through the decimal representation of the addresses of the nodes. Let $N=2^n$ be the number of nodes and i represent the decimal address of a node.

Mesh: It is a two dimensional network. In this all processing elements are arranged in a two dimensional grid. The processor in rows i and column j are denoted by PE_i.

The processors on the corner can communicate to two nearest neighbors i.e. PE_{00} can communicate with PE_{01} and PE_{10} . The processor on the boundary can communicate to 3 adjacent processing elements i.e. PE_{01} can communicate with PE_{00}, PE_{02} and PE_{11} and internally placed processors can communicate with 4 adjacent processors i.e. PE_{11} can communicate with PE_{01}, PE_{10}, PE_{12}, and PE_{21}

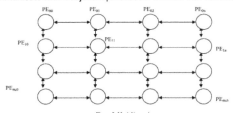

Two-dimensional mesh. A two- dimensional mesh consists of $k_1 \ast k_0$ nodes, where $k_i \geq 2$ denotes the number of nodes along dimension i. Figure 11 represents a two-dimensional mesh for $k_0=4$ and $k_1=2$. There are four nodes along dimension 0, and two nodes along dimension 1. As shown in Figure 5.11, in a two-dimensional mesh network each node is connected to its north, south, east, and west neighbors. In general, a node at row i and column j is connected to the nodes at locations $(i\text{-}1, j)$, $(i\text{+}1, j)$, $(i, j\text{-}1)$, and $(i, j\text{+}1)$. The nodes on the edge of the network have only two or three immediate neighbors.

The diameter of a mesh network is equal to the distance between nodes at opposite corners. Thus, a two-dimensional mesh with $k_1 \ast k_0$ nodes has a diameter $(k_1 -1) + (k_0\text{-}1)$.

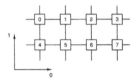

Figure 11 A two-dimensional mesh with $k_0=4$ and $k_1=2$.

In practice, two-dimensional meshes with an equal number of nodes along each dimension are often used for connecting a set of processing nodes. For this reason in most literature the notion of two-dimensional mesh is used without indicating the values for k_1 and k_0; rather, the total number of nodes is defined. A two-dimensional mesh with $k_1=k_0=n$ is usually referred to as a *mesh* with N nodes, where $N = n^2$. For example,

Figure 12 shows a mesh with 16 nodes. From this point forward, the term *mesh* will indicated a two-dimensional mesh with an equal number of nodes along each dimension.

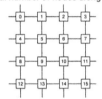

Figure 12 A two-dimensional mesh with $k_0=k_1=4$.

It should be noted that in the case just described the nodes on the edge of the mesh network have no connections to their far neighbors. When there are such connections, the network is called a *wraparound* two-dimensional mesh, or an ***Illiac*** network. An Illiac network is illustrated in Figure 13 for $N = 16$.

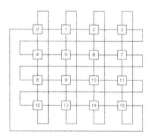

Figure 13 A 16-node Illiac network.

In general, the connections of an Illiac network can be defined by the following four functions:

$$\text{Illiac}_{+1}(j) = j+1 \pmod N,$$
$$\text{Illiac}_{-1}(j) = j-1 \pmod N,$$
$$\text{Illiac}_{+n}(j) = j+n \pmod N,$$
$$\text{Illiac}_{-n}(j) = j-n \pmod N,$$

where N is the number of nodes, $0 \le j < N$, n is the number of nodes along any dimension, and $N=n^2$. For example, in Figure 5.14, node 4 is connected to nodes 5, 3, 8, and 0, since

$$\text{Illiac}_{+1}(4) = (4+1) \pmod{16} = 5,$$
$$\text{Illiac}_{-1}(4) = (4-1) \pmod{16} = 3,$$
$$\text{Illiac}_{+4}(4) = (4+4) \pmod{16} = 8,$$
$$\text{Illiac}_{-4}(4) = (4-4) \pmod{16} = 0.$$

The diameter of an Illiac with $N=n^2$ nodes is n-1, which is shorter than a mesh. Although the extra wraparound connections in Illiac allow the diameter to decrease, they increase the complexity of the design.

Figure 14 shows the connectivity of the nodes in a different form. This graph shows that four nodes can be reached from any node in one step, seven nodes in two steps, and four nodes in three steps. In general, the number of steps (recirculations) to route data from a node to any other node is upper bounded by the diameter (i.e., $n - 1$).

Figure 14 Alternative representation of a 16-node Illiac network.

Cube: It is a 3 dimensional interconnection network. In this the PE's are arranged

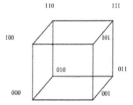

n-cube or hypercube. An n-cube network, also called hypercube, consists of $N=2^n$ nodes; n is called the *dimension* of the n-cube network. When the node addresses are considered as the corners of an n-dimensional cube, the network connects each node to its n neighbors. In an n-cube, individual nodes are uniquely identified by n-bit addresses ranging from 0 to N-1. Given a node with binary address d, this node is connected to all nodes whose binary addresses differ from d in exactly 1 bit. For example, in a 3-cube, in which there are eight nodes, node 7 (111) is connected to nodes 6 (110), 5 (101), and 3 (011). Figure 16 demonstrates all the connections between the nodes.

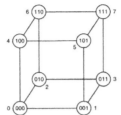

Figure 16 A three-dimensional cube.

Different networks, such as two-dimensional meshes and trees, can be embedded in an *n*-cube in such a way that the connectivity between neighboring nodes remains consistent with their definition. Figure 17 shows how a 4-by-4 mesh can be embedded in a 4- cube (four-dimensional hypercube). The 4-cube's integrity is not compromised and is well-suited for uses like this, where a great deal of flexibility is required. All definitional considerations for both the 4-cube and the 4-by-4 mesh, as stated earlier, are consistent.

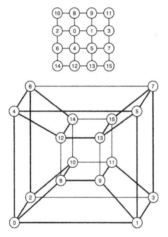

Figure 17 Embedding a 4-by-4 mesh in a 4-cube.

Systolic Array: This interconnection network is a type of pipelined array architecture and it is designed for multidimensional flow of data. It is used for implementing fixed algorithms. Systolic array designed for performing matrix multiplication is shown below. All interior nodes have degree 6.

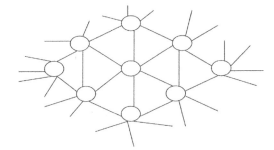

Figure 18: Systolic Array

Dynamic Networks

Dynamic networks provide reconfigurable connections between nodes. The topology of a dynamic network is the physical structure of the network as determined by the switch boxes and the interconnecting links. Since the switch box is the basic component of the network, the cost of the network (in hardware terms) is measured by the number of switch boxes required. Therefore, the topology of the network is the prime determinant of the cost.

To clarify the preceding terminology, let us consider the design of a dynamic network using simple switch boxes. Figure 19 represents a simple switch with two inputs (x and y) and two outputs (z_0 and z_1). A control line, s, determines whether the input lines should be connected to the output lines in straight state or exchange state. For example, when the control line $s=0$, the inputs are connected to the outputs in a straight state; that is, x is connected to z_0 and y is connected to z_1. When the control line $s=1$, the inputs are connected to outputs in an exchange state; that is, x is connected to z_1 and y is connected to z_0.

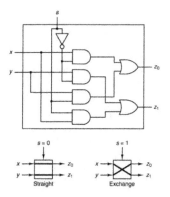

Figure 19 A simple two-input switch.

Now let's use this switch to design a network that can connect a source x to one of eight possible destinations 0 to 7. A solution for such a network is shown in Figure 20. In this design, there are three stages (columns), stages 2, 1, and 0. The destination address is denoted bit-wise $d_2 d_1 d_0$. The switch in stage 2 is controlled by the most significant bit of the destination address (i.e., d_2).

This bit is used because, when $d_2=0$, the source x is connected to one of the destinations 0 to 3 (000 to 011); otherwise, x is connected to one of the destinations 4 to 7 (100 to 111). In a similar way, the switches in stages 1 and 0 are controlled by d_1 and d_0, respectively.

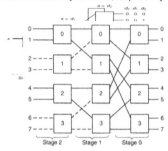

Figure 20 A simple 1-to-8 interconnection network.

Now let's expand our network to have eight sources instead of one. Figure 5.35 represents a solution to such a network constructed in the same manner as the design in Figure 20.

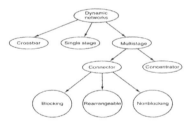

Figure 21 A simple 8-to-8 interconnection network.

Classification of dynamic networks.

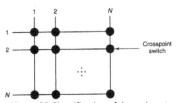

Figure 22 Classification of dynamic networks.

The crossbar switch can be used for connecting a set of input nodes to a set of output nodes. In this network every input node can be connected to any output node. The crossbar switch provides all possible permutations, as well as support for high system performance. It can be viewed as a number of vertical and horizontal links interconnected by a switch at each intersection. Figure 23 represents a crossbar for connecting N nodes to N nodes. The connection between each pair of nodes is established by a crosspoint switch. The crosspoint switch can be set on or off in response to application needs. There are N^2 crosspoint switches for providing complete connections between all the nodes. The crossbar switch is an ideal network to use for small N. However, for large N, the implementation of the crosspoint switches makes this design complex and expensive and thus less attractive to use.

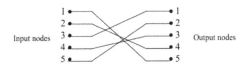

Figure 23 Crossbar switch.

CONCEPT OF PERMUTATION NETWORK
In permutation interconnection networks the information exchange requires data transfer from input set of nodes to output set of nodes and possible connections between edges are established by applying various permutations in available links. There are various networks where multiple paths from source to destination are possible. For finding out what the possible routes in such networks are the study of the permutation concept is a must.

Let us look at the basic concepts of permutation with respect to interconnection network.
Let us say the network has set of n input nodes and n output nodes.
Permutation P for a network of 5 nodes (i.e., n = 5) is written as follows:

$$P = \frac{1\ 2\ 3\ 4\ 5}{5\ 4\ 1\ 3\ 2}$$

It means node connections are $1 \leftrightarrow 5, 2 \leftrightarrow 4, 3 \leftrightarrow 1, 4 \leftrightarrow 3, 5 \leftrightarrow 2$.

The connections are shown in the *Figure 24.*

The other permutation of the same set of nodes may be

$$P = \begin{bmatrix} 1 & 2 & 3 & 4 & 5 \\ 2 & 3 & 5 & 1 & 4 \end{bmatrix}$$

Which means connections are: $1\leftrightarrow2$, $2\leftrightarrow3$, $3\leftrightarrow5$, $4\leftrightarrow1$, and $5\leftrightarrow4$
Similarly, other permutations are also possible. The Set of all permutations of a 3-node network will be

$$P = \begin{bmatrix} 1 & 2 & 3 \\ 1 & 3 & 2 \end{bmatrix}, \begin{bmatrix} 1 & 2 & 3 \\ 2 & 1 & 3 \end{bmatrix}, \begin{bmatrix} 1 & 2 & 3 \\ 2 & 3 & 1 \end{bmatrix}, \begin{bmatrix} 1 & 2 & 3 \\ 3 & 1 & 2 \end{bmatrix}, \begin{bmatrix} 1 & 2 & 3 \\ 3 & 2 & 1 \end{bmatrix}$$

Connection, $\begin{bmatrix} 1 & 2 & 3 \\ 1 & 2 & 3 \end{bmatrix}$ indicates connection from node 1 to node1, node 2 to node 2, and node 3 to node 3, hence it has no meaning, so it is dropped.

In these examples, only one set of links exist between input and output nodes and means it is a single stage network. It may be possible that there exist multiple links between input and output (i.e. multistage network). Permutation of all these in a multistage network are called permutation group and these are represented by a cycle e.g. permutation

P= (1,2,3) (4,5) means the network has two groups of input and output nodes, one group consists of nodes 1,2,3 and another group consists of nodes 4,5 and connections are $1 \to 2$, $2 \to 3$, $3 \to 1$, and $4 \to 5$. Here group (1,2,3) has period 3 and (4,5) has period 2, collectively these groups has periodicity 3×2=6.

Interconnection from all the possible input nodes to all the output nodes forms the permutation group. There are few permutations of special significance in interconnection network. These permutations are provided by hardware. Now, let us discuss these permutations in detail.

1) **Perfect Shuffle Permutation:** This was suggested by Harold Stone (1971). Consider N objects each represented by n bit number say X_{n-1}, X_{n-2}, X_0 (N is chosen such that N = 2n.) The perfect shuffle of these N objects is expressed as

$$X_{n-1}, X_{n-2}, X_0 = X_{n-2}, X_0\ X_{n-1}.$$

That, means perfect shuffle is obtained by rotating the address by 1 bit left. e.g. shuffle of 8 objects is shown as

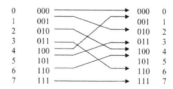

2) **Butterfly permutation:** This permutation is obtained by interchanging the most significant bit in address with least significant bit.

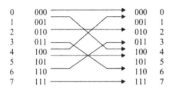

An interconnection network based on this permutation is the butterfly network. A butterfly network is a blocking network and it does not allow an arbitrary connection of N inputs to N outputs without conflict. The butterfly network is modified in Benz network. The Benz network is a non-blocking network and it is generated by joining two butterfly networks back to back, in such a manner that data flows forward through one and in reverse through the other.

3) **Clos network:** This network was developed by Clos (1953). It is a non-blocking network and provides full connectivity like crossbar network but it requires significantly less number of switches. The organization of Clos network is shown in *Figure 19:*

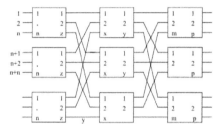

Consider an I input and O output network
Number N is chosen such that (I= n.x) and (O=p.y).

In Clos network input stage will consist of X switches each having n input lines and z output lines. The last stage will consist of Y switches each having m input lines and p output lines and the middle stage will consist of z crossbar switches, each of size X × Y. To utilize all inputs the value of Z is kept greater than or equal to n and p.

The connection between various stages is made as follows: all outputs of 1st crossbar switch of first stage are joined with 1st input of all switches of middle stage. (i.e., 1st output of first page with 1st middle stage, 2nd output of first stage with 1st input of second switch of middle stage and so on...)

The outputs of second switch of first stage. Stage are joined with 2nd input of various switches of second stage (i.e., 1st output of second switch of 1st stage is joined with 2 input of 1st switch of middle stage and 2nd output of 2 nd switch of 1st stage is joined with 2nd input of 2nd switch of middle stage and so on...

Similar connections are made between middle stage and output stage (i.e. outputs of 1st switch of middle stage are connected with 1st input of various switches of third stage.

Permutation matrix of P in the above example the matrix entries will be n

Bens Network: It is a non-blocking network. It is a special type of Clos network where first and last stage consists of 2×2 switches (for n input and m output network it will have n/2 switches of 2 ×2

order and the last stage will have m/2 switch of 2×2 order the middle stage will have two n/2 X m/2 switches. Numbers n and m are assumed to be the power of 2.

Thus, for 16×16 3-stage Bens network first stage and third stage will consist of 8 (2×2) switches and middle stage will consist of 2 switches of size (8×8). The connection of crossbar will be as follows:

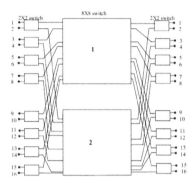

The switches of various stages provide complete connectivity. Thus by properly configuring the switch any input can be passed to any output.

INTERCONNECTION DESIGN DECISIONS

A major problem in parallel computer design is finding an interconnection network capable of providing fast and efficient communication at a reasonable cost. There are at least five design considerations when selecting the architecture of an interconnection network: operation mode, switching methodology, network topology, a control strategy, and the functional characteristics of the switch.

Operation mode. Three primary operating modes are available to the interconnection network designer: synchronous, asynchronous, and combined. When a synchronous stream of instructions or data is required by the network, a synchronous communication system is required. In other words, synchronous communication is needed for establishing communication paths synchronously for either data manipulating functions or for a data instruction broadcast. Most SIMD machines operate in a lock -step fashion; that is, all active processing nodes transmit data at the same time. Thus synchronous communication seems an appropriate choice for SIMD machines.

When connection requests for an interconnection network are issued dynamically, an asynchronous communication system is needed. Since the timing of the routing requests is not predictable, the system must be able to handle such requests at any time.

Some systems are designed to handle both synchronous and asynchronous communications. Such systems are able to do array processing by utilizing synchronous communications, yet are also able to control less predictable communication requests by using asynchronous timing methods.

Switching methodology. The three main types of switching methodologies are circuit switching, packet switching, and integrated switching. Circuit switching establishes a complete path between source and destination and holds this path for the entire transmission. It is best suited for transmitting large amounts of continuous data. In contrast to circuit switching, packet switching has no dedicated physical connection set up. Hence it is most useful for transmitting small amounts of data. In packet switching, data items are partitioned into fixed -size packets. Each packet has a header that contains routing information, and moves from one node in the network to the next. The packet switching increases channel throughput by multiplexing various packets through the same path. Most SIMD machines use circuit switching, while packet switching is most suited to MIMD machines.

The third option, integrated switching, is a combination of circuit and packet switching. This allows large amounts of data to be moved quickly over the physical path while allowing smaller packets of information to be transmitted via the network.

Network topology. To design or select a topology, several performance parameters should be considered. The most important parameters are the following.

VLSI implementable. The topology of the network should be able to be mapped on two (or three) physical dimensions so that it can produce an efficient layout for packaging and implementation in
VLSI systems.
Small diameter. the diameter of the network should grow slowly with the number of nodes.
Neighbor independancy. The number of neighbors of any node should be independent of the size of the network. This allows the network to scale up to a very large size.
Easy to route. There should be an efficient algorithm for routing messages from any node to any other. The messages must find an optimal path between the source and destination nodes and make use of all of the available bandwidth.
Uniform load. The traffic load on various parts of the network should be uniform.
Redundant Pathways. The network should be highly reliable and highly available. Message pathways should be redundant to provide robustness in the event of component failure.

PERFORMANCE METRICS

The performance of interconnection networks is measured on the following parameters.

Bandwidth: It is a measure of maximum transfer rate between two nodes. It is measured in Megabytes per second or Gigabytes per second.

Functionality: It indicates how interconnection networks supports data routing, interrupt handling, synchronization, request/message combining and coherence.

Latency: In interconnection networks various nodes may be at different distances depending upon the topology. The network latency refers to the worst-case time delay for a unit message when transferred through the network between farthest nodes.

Scalability: It refers to the ability of interconnection networks for modular expansion with a scalable performance with increasing machine resources.

Hardware Complexity: It refers to the cost of hardware logic like wires, connectors, switches, arbiter etc. that are required for implementation of interconnection network.

4

PARALLEL COMPUTER ARCHITECTURE

Introduction
Pipeline Processing
        Classification of Pipeline Processors
            Instruction Pipelines
            Arithmetic Pipelines
        Performance and Issues in Pipelining
Vector Processing
Array Processing
        Associative Array Processing
Multi-threaded Processors

INTRODUCTION

In this unit, various parallel architectures are discussed, which are based on the classification of parallel computers considered earlier. The two major parametric considerations in designing a parallel computer architecture are: (i) executing multiple number of instructions in parallel, and (ii) increasing the efficiency of processors. There are various methods by which instructions can be executed in parallel and parallel architectures are based on these methods of executing instructions in parallel. Pipelining is one of the classical and effective methods to increase parallelism where different stages perform repeated functions on different operands. Vector processing is the arithmetic or logical computation applied on vectors whereas in scalar processing only one data item or a pair of data items is processed. Parallel architectures have also been developed based on associative memory organizations. Another idea of improving the processor's speed by having multiple instructions per cycle is known as Superscalar processing. Multithreading for increasing processor utilization has also been used in parallel computer architecture. All the architectures based on these parallel-processing types have been discussed in detail in this unit.

PIPELINE PROCESSING

Pipelining is a method to realize, overlapped parallelism in the proposed solution of a problem, on a digital computer in an economical way. To understand the concept of pipelining, we need to understand first the concept of assembly lines in an automated production plant where items are assembled from separate parts (stages) and output of one stage becomes the input to another stage. Taking the analogy of assembly lines, pipelining is the method to introduce temporal parallelism in computer operations. Assembly line is the pipeline and the separate parts of the assembly line are different stages through which operands of an operation are passed.

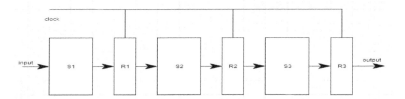

To introduce pipelining in a processor P, the following steps must be followed:

- Sub-divide the input process into a sequence of subtasks. These subtasks will make stages of pipeline, which are also known as segments.
-
- Each stage S_i of the pipeline according to the subtask will perform some operation on a distinct set of operands.
- When stage S_i has completed its operation, results are passed to the next stage S_{i+1} for the next operation.
- The stage S_i receives a new set of input from previous stage S_{i-1} .

In this way, parallelism in a pipelined processor can be achieved such that m independent operations can be performed simultaneously in m segments as shown in *Figure 1*.

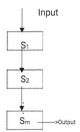

Figure 1: m-Segment Pipeline Processor

The stages or segments are implemented as pure combinational circuits performing arithmetic or logic operations over the data streams flowing through the pipe. Latches are used to separate the stages, which are fast registers to hold intermediate results between the stages as shown in *Figure 2*. Each stage S_i consists of a latch L_i and a processing circuit C_i. The final output is stored in output register R. The flow of data from one stage to another is controlled by a common clock.

Thus, in each clock period, one stage transfers its results to another stage.

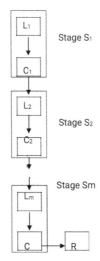

Figure 2: Pipelined Processor

Pipelined Processor: Having discussed pipelining, now we can define a pipeline processor. A pipeline processor can be defined as a processor that consists of a sequence of processing circuits called segments and a stream of operands (data) is passed through the pipeline. In each segment partial processing of the data stream is performed and the final output is received when the stream has passed through the whole pipeline. An operation that can be decomposed into a sequence of well-defined sub tasks is realized through the pipelining concept.

Classification of Pipeline Processors

In this section, we describe various types of pipelining that can be applied in computer operations. These types depend on the following factors:

- Level of Processing
- Pipeline configuration
- Type of Instruction and data

Classification according to level of processing

According to this classification, computer operations are classified as instruction execution and arithmetic operations. Next, we discuss these classes of this classification:

1) **Instruction Pipeline:** We know that an instruction cycle may consist of many operations like, fetch opcode, decode opcode, compute operand addresses, fetch operands, and execute instructions. These operations of the instruction execution cycle can be realized through the pipelining concept. Each of these operations forms one stage of a pipeline. The overlapping of execution of the operations through the pipeline provides a speedup over the normal execution. Thus, the pipelines used for instruction cycle operations are known as *instruction pipelines.*

2) **Arithmetic Pipeline:** The complex arithmetic operations like multiplication, and floating point operations consume much of the time of the ALU. These operations can also be pipelined by segmenting the operations of the ALU and as a consequence, high speed performance may be achieved. Thus, the pipelines used for arithmetic operations are known as *arithmetic pipelines.*

Classification according to pipeline configuration:
According to the configuration of a pipeline, the following types are identified under this classification:

- **Unifunction Pipelines**: When a fixed and dedicated function is performed through a pipeline, it is called a Unifunction pipeline.

- **Multifunction Pipelines**: When different functions at different times are performed through the pipeline, this is known as Multifunction pipeline. Multifunction pipelines are reconfigurable at different times according to the operation being performed.

Classification according to type of instruction and data:
According to the types of instruction and data, following types are identified under this classification:

- **Scalar Pipelines**: This type of pipeline processes scalar operands of repeated scalar instructions.

- **Vector Pipelines:** This type of pipeline processes vector instructions over vector operands.

Instruction Pipelines

As discussed earlier, the stream of instructions in the instruction execution cycle, can be realized through a pipeline where overlapped execution of different operations are performed. The process of executing the instruction involves the following major steps:

- Fetch the instruction from the main memory
- Decode the instruction
- Fetch the operand
- Execute the decoded instruction

These four steps become the candidates for stages for the pipeline, which we call as instruction pipeline (It is shown in *Figure 3*).

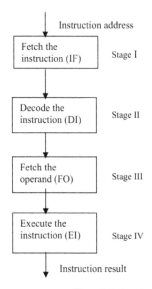

Figure 3: Instruction Pipeline

Since, in the pipelined execution, there is overlapped execution of operations, the four stages of the instruction pipeline will work in the overlapped manner. First, the instruction address is fetched from the memory to the first stage of the pipeline. The first stage fetches the instruction and gives its output to the second stage. While the second stage of the pipeline is decoding the instruction, the first stage gets another input and fetches the next instruction. When the first instruction has been decoded in the second stage, then its output is fed to the third stage. When the third stage is fetching the operand for the first instruction, then the second stage gets the second instruction and the first stage gets input for another instruction and so on. In this way, the pipeline is executing the instruction in an overlapped manner increasing the throughput and speed of execution.

The scenario of these overlapped operations in the instruction pipeline can be illustrated through the space-time diagram. In *Figure 4*, first we show the space-time diagram for non-overlapped execution in a sequential environment and then for the overlapped pipelined environment. It is clear from the two diagrams that in non-overlapped execution, results are achieved only after 4 cycles while in overlapped pipelined execution, after 4 cycles, we are getting output after each cycle. Soon in the instruction pipeline, the instruction cycle has been reduced to ¼ of the sequential execution.

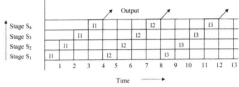

Figure 4(a) Space-time diagram for Non-pipelined Processor

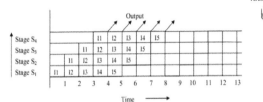

Figure 4(b) Space-time diagram for Overlapped Instruction pipelined Processor

Instruction buffers: For taking the full advantage of pipelining, pipelines should be filled continuously. Therefore, instruction fetch rate should be matched with the pipeline consumption rate. To do this, instruction buffers are used. Instruction buffers in CPU have high speed memory for storing the instructions. The instructions are pre-fetched in the buffer from the main memory. Another alternative for the instruction buffer is the cache memory between the CPU and the main memory. The advantage of cache memory is that it can be used for both instruction and data. But cache requires more complex control logic than the instruction buffer. Some pipelined computers have adopted both.

Arithmetic Pipelines

The technique of pipelining can be applied to various complex and slow arithmetic operations to speed up the processing time. The pipelines used for arithmetic computations are called *Arithmetic pipelines*. In this section, we discuss arithmetic pipelines based on arithmetic operations. Arithmetic pipelines are constructed for simple fixed-point and complex floating-point arithmetic operations. These arithmetic operations are well suited to pipelining as these operations can be efficiently partitioned into subtasks for the pipeline stages. For implementing the arithmetic pipelines we generally use following two types of adder:

> **Carry propagation adder (CPA)**: It adds two numbers such that carries generated in successive digits are propagated.

> **Carry save adder (CSA)**: It adds two numbers such that carries generated are not propagated rather these are saved in a carry vector.

Fixed Arithmetic pipelines: We take the example of multiplication of fixed numbers. Two fixed -point numbers are added by the ALU using add and shift operations. This sequential execution makes the multiplication a slow process. If we look at the multiplication process carefully, then we observe that this is the process of adding the multiple copies of shifted multiplicands as show below:

$$
\begin{array}{cccccc}
X_5 & X_4 & X_3 & X_2 & X_1 & X_0 & = X
\end{array}
$$

$$
\begin{array}{cccccc}
Y_5 & Y_4 & Y_3 & Y_2 & Y_1 & Y_0 & = Y
\end{array}
$$

$$X_5Y_0 \ X_4Y_0 \ X_3Y_0 \ X_2Y_0 \ X_1Y_0 \ X_0Y_0 = P_1$$

$$X_5Y_1 \ X_4Y_1 \ X_3Y_1 \ X_2Y_1 \ X_1Y_1 \ X_0Y_1 \quad = P_2$$

$$X_5Y_2 \ X_4Y_2 \ X_3Y_2 \ X_2Y_2 \ X_1Y_2 \ X_0Y_2 \quad = P_3$$

$$X_5Y_3 \ X_4Y_3 \ X_3Y_3 \ X_2Y_3 \ X_1Y_3 \ X_0Y_3 \quad = P_4$$

$$X_5Y_4 \ X_4Y_4 \ X_3Y_4 \ X_2Y_4 \ X_1Y_4 \ X_0Y_4 \quad = P_5$$

$$X_5Y_5 \ X_4Y_5 \ X_3Y_5 \ X_2Y_5 \ X_1Y_5 \ X_0Y_5 \quad = P_6$$

Now, we can identify the following stages for the pipeline:

The first stage generates the partial product of the numbers, which form the six rows of shifted multiplicands.

In the second stage, the six numbers are given to the two CSAs merging into four numbers.

In the third stage, there is a single CSA merging the numbers into 3 numbers.

In the fourth stage, there is a single number merging three numbers into 2 numbers.

In the fifth stage, the last two numbers are added through a CPA to get the final product.

These stages have been implemented using CSA tree as shown in *Figure 5*.

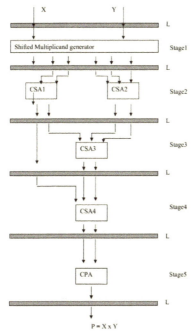

Figure 5: Arithmetic pipeline for Multiplication of two 6-digit fixed numbers

Floating point Arithmetic pipelines: Floating point computations are the best candidates for pipelining. Take the example of addition of two floating point numbers. Following stages are identified for the addition of two floating point numbers:

- First stage will compare the exponents of the two numbers.
- Second stage will look for alignment of mantissas.
- In the third stage, mantissas are added.
- In the last stage, the result is normalized.

These stages are shown in *Figure 6*.

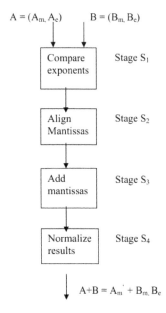

$A = (A_m, A_e)$ $B = (B_m, B_e)$

Compare exponents	Stage S_1
Align Mantissas	Stage S_2
Add mantissas	Stage S_3
Normalize results	Stage S_4

$A+B = A_m' + B_m. B_e$

Figure 6: Arithmetic Pipeline for Floating point addition of two numbers

Performance and Issues in Pipelining

Speedup : First we take the speedup factor that is we see how much speed up performance we get through pipelining.

First we take the *ideal case* for measuring the speedup.

Let n be the total number of tasks executed through m stages of pipelines.

Then m stages can process n tasks in clock cycles = m + (n-1) Time taken to execute without pipelining = m.n

Speedup due to pipelining = m.n/[m +(n-1)].

As n>=∞ , There is speedup of n times over the non-pipelined execution.

Efficiency: The efficiency of a pipeline can be measured as the ratio of busy time span to the total time span including the idle time. Let c be the clock period of the pipeline, the efficiency E can be denoted as:

$$E = (n. m. c) / m.[m.c + (n-1).c] = n / (m + (n-1)$$

As n-> ∞ , E becomes 1.

Throughput: Throughput of a pipeline can be defined as the number of results that have been achieved per unit time. It can be denoted as:

$$T = n / [m + (n-1)]. c = E / c$$

Throughput denotes the computing power of the pipeline.

Maximum speedup, efficiency and throughput are the ideal cases but these are not achieved in the practical cases, as the speedup is limited due to the following factors:

- **Data dependency between successive tasks:** There may be dependencies between the instructions of two tasks used in the pipeline. For example, one instruction cannot be started until the previous instruction returns the results, as both are interdependent. Another instance of data dependency will be when that both instructions try to modify the same data object. These are called *data hazards*.

- **Resource Constraints:** When resources are not available at the time of execution then delays are caused in pipelining. For example, if one common memory is used for both data and instructions and there is need to read/write and fetch the instruction at the same time then only one can be carried out and the other has to wait. Another example is of limited resource like execution unit, which may be busy at the required time.

- **Branch Instructions and Interrupts in the program:** A program is not a straight flow of sequential instructions. There may be branch instructions that alter the normal flow of program, which delays the pipelining execution and affects the performance. Similarly, there are interrupts that postpones the execution of next instruction until the interrupt has been serviced. Branches and the interrupts have damaging effects on the pipelining.

Advantages of Pipelining

1. The cycle time of the processor is reduced.
2. It increases the throughput of the system
3. It makes the system reliable.

Disadvantages of Pipelining

1. The design of pipelined processor is complex and costly to manufacture.
2. The instruction latency is more.

Parallelism vs Pipelining

Parallel computing is the simultaneous execution of the same task (split up and specially adapted) on multiple processors in order to obtain results faster. The idea is based on the fact that the process of solving a problem usually can be divided into smaller tasks, which may be carried out simultaneously with some coordination.

A parallel computing system is a computer with more than one processor for parallel processing. In the past, each processor of a multiprocessing system always came in its own processor packaging, but recently-introduced multicore processors contain multiple logical processors in a single package.

There are many different kinds of parallel computers. They are distinguished by the kind of interconnection between processors (known as "processing elements" or PEs) and memory.

Pipelining is a method of increasing system performance and throughput. It takes advantage of the inherent parallelism in instructions. Instructions are divided into 5 stages : IF, ID, EX, MEM, WB. In pipelining, we try to execute 2 or more instructions at the same time thereby increasing the throughput.

VECTOR PROCESSING

A *vector* is an ordered set of the same type of scalar data items. The scalar item can be a floating pint number, an integer or a logical value. *Vector processing* is the arithmetic or logical computation applied on vectors whereas in scalar processing only one or pair of data is processed. Therefore, vector processing is faster compared to scalar processing. When the scalar code is converted to vector form then it is called v*ectorization*. A *vector processor* is a special coprocessor, which is designed to handle the vector computations.

Vector instructions can be classified as below:

- **Vector-Vector Instructions**: In this type, vector operands are fetched from the vector register and stored in another vector register. These instructions are denoted with the following function mappings:

  F1 : V -> V
  F2 : V × V -> V

  For example, vector square root is of F1 type and addition of two vectors is of F2.
- **Vector-Scalar Instructions**: In this type, when the combination of scalar and vector are fetched and stored in vector register. These instructions are denoted with the following function mappings:

  F3 : S × V -> V where S is the scalar item
  For example, vector-scalar addition or divisions are of F3 type.
- **Vector reduction Instructions**: When operations on vector are being reduced to scalar items as the result, then these are vector reduction instructions. These instructions are denoted with the following function mappings:

  F4 : V -> S
  F5 : V × V -> S

  For example, finding the maximum, minimum and summation of all the elements of vector are of the type F4. The dot product of two vectors is generated by F5.

- **Vector-Memory Instructions**: When vector operations with memory M are performed then these are vector-memory instructions. These instructions are denoted with the following function mappings:

  F6 : M-> V
  F7 : V -> V

For example, vector load is of type F6 and vector store operation is of F7.

- **Vector Processing with Pipelining**: Since in vector processing, vector instructions perform the same computation on different data operands repeatedly, vector processing is most suitable for pipelining. Vector processors with pipelines are designed to handle vectors of varying length n where n is the length of vector. A vector processor performs better if length of vector is larger. But large values of n causes the problem in storage of vectors and there is difficulty in moving the vectors to and from the pipelines.

Pipeline Vector processors adopt the following two architectural configurations for this problem as discussed below:

> *Memory-to-Memory Architecture*: The pipelines can access vector operands, intermediate and final results directly in the main memory. This requires the higher memory bandwidth. Moreover, the information of the base address, the offset and vector length should be specified for transferring the data streams between the main memory and pipelines. STAR-100 and TI-ASC computers have adopted this architecture for vector instructions.

> *Register*-to-**Register** Architecture: In this organization, operands and results are accessed indirectly from the main memory through the scalar or vector registers. The vectors which are required currently can be stored in the CPU registers. Cray-1 computer adopts this architecture for the vector instructions and its CPY contains 8 vector registers, each register capable of storing a 64 element vector where one element is of 8 bytes.

Efficiency of Vector Processing over Scalar Processing:

As we know, a sequential computer processes scalar operands one at a time. Therefore if we have to process a vector of length n through the sequential computer then the vector must be broken into n scalar steps and executed one by one.
For example, consider the following vector addition:

$$A + B \rightarrow C$$

The vectors are of length 500. This operation through the sequential computer can be specified by 500 add instructions as given below:

$$C[1] = A[1] + B[1]$$
$$C[2] = A[2] + B[2]$$
$$C[500] = A[500] + B[500]$$

If we perform the same operation through a pipelined-vector computer then it does not break the vectors in 500 add statements. Because a vector processor has the set of vector instructions that allow the operations to be specified in one vector instruction as:

$$A\ (1{:}500) + B\ (1{:}500) \rightarrow C\ (1{:}500)$$

Each vector operation may be broken internally in scalar operations but they are executed in parallel which results in mush faster execution as compared to sequential computer.

Thus, the advantage of adopting vector processing over scalar processing is that it eliminates the overhead caused by the loop control required in a sequential computer.

ARRAY PROCESSING

We have seen that for performing vector operations, the pipelining concept has been used. There is another method for vector operations. If we have an array of n processing elements (PEs) i.e., multiple ALUs for storing multiple operands of the vector, then an n instruction, for example, vector addition, is broadcast to all PEs such that they add all operands of the vector at the same time. That means all PEs will perform computation in parallel. All PEs are synchronised under one control unit.

This organisation of synchronous array of PEs for vector operations is called *Array Processor*. The organisation is same as in SIMD which we studied in unit 2. An array processor can handle one instruction and multiple data streams as we have seen in case of SIMD organisation. Therefore, array processors are also called *SIMD array computers*.

The organisation of an array processor is shown in *Figure 7.* The following components are organised in an array processor:

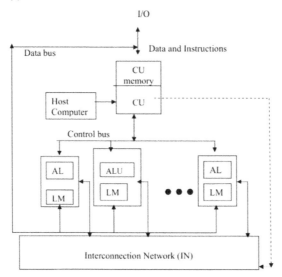

Figure 7: Organisation of SIMD Array Processor

Control Unit (CU) : All PEs are under the control of one control unit. CU controls the inter communication between the PEs. There is a local memory of CU also called CY memory. The user programs are loaded into the CU memory. The vector instructions in the program are decoded by CU and broadcast to the array of PEs. Instruction fetch and decoding is done by the CU only.

Processing elements (PEs) : Each processing element consists of ALU, its registers and a local memory for storage of distributed data. These PEs have been interconnected via an interconnection network. All PEs receive the instructions from the control unit and the different component operands are fetched from their local memory. Thus, all PEs perform the same function synchronously in a lock-step fashion under the control of the CU.

It may be possible that all PEs need not participate in the execution of a vector instruction. Therefore, it is required to adopt a masking scheme to control the status of each PE. A *masking vector* is used to control the status of all PEs such that only enabled PEs are allowed to participate in the execution and others are disabled.

Interconnection Network (IN): IN performs data exchange among the PEs, data routing and manipulation functions. This IN is under the control of CU.

Host Computer: An array processor may be attached to a host computer through the control unit. The purpose of the host computer is to broadcast a sequence of vector instructions through CU to the PEs. Thus, the host computer is a general-purpose machine that acts as a manager of the entire system.

Array processors are special purpose computers which have been adopted for the following:

- various scientific applications,
- matrix algebra,
- matrix eigen value calculations,
- real-time scene analysis

SIMD array processor on the large scale has been developed by NASA for earth resources satellite image processing. This computer has been named *Massively parallel processor* (MPP) because it contains 16,384 processors that work in parallel. MPP provides real-time time varying scene analysis.

However, array processors are not commercially popular and are not commonly used. The reasons are that array processors are difficult to program compared to pipelining and there is problem in vectorization.

Associative Array Processing

Consider that a table or a list of record is stored in the memory and you want to find some information in that list. For example, the list consists of three fields as shown below:

Name	ID Number	Age
Sumit	234	23
Ramesh	136	26
Ravi	97	35

Suppose now that we want to find the ID number and age of Ravi. If we use conventional RAM then it is necessary to give the exact physical address of entry related to Ravi in the instruction access the entry such as:

      READ ROW 3

Another alternative idea is that we search the whole list using the Name field as an address in the instruction such as:

      READ NAME = RAVI

Again with serial access memory this option can be implemented easily but it is a very slow process. An **associative memory** helps at this point and simultaneously examines all the entries in the list and returns the desired list very quickly.

SIMD array computers have been developed with *associative memory*. An associative memory is content addressable memory, by which it is meant that multiple memory words are accessible in parallel. The parallel accessing feature also support parallel search and parallel compare. This capability can be used in many applications such as:

- Storage and retrieval of databases which are changing rapidly
- Radar signal tracking
- Image processing
- Artificial Intelligence

The inherent parallelism feature of this memory has great advantages and impact in parallel computer architecture. The associative memory is costly compared to RAM. The array processor built with associative memory is called *Associative array processor*. In this section, we describe some categories of associative array processor. Types of associative processors are based on the organisation of associative memory. Therefore, first we discuss about the associative memory organisation.

Associative Memory Organisations

The associative memory is organised in *w* words with *b* bits per word. In w x b array, each bit is called a *cell*. Each cell is made up of a flip-flop that contains some comparison logic gates for pattern match and read-write operations. Therefore, it is possible to read or write in parallel due to this logic structure.

A group of bit cells of all the words at the same position in a vertical column is called *bit slice* as shown in *Figure 8*.

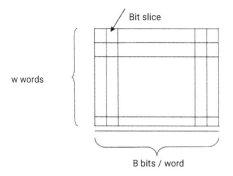

Figure 8: Associative memory

In the organisation of an associative memory, following registers are used:

Comparand Register (C): This register is used to hold the operands, which are being searched for, or being compared with.

Masking Register (M): It may be possible that all bit slices are not involved in parallel operations. Masking register is used to enable or disable the bit slices.

Indicator (I) and *Temporary* (T) *Registers*: Indicator register is used to hold the current match patterns and temporary registers are used to hold the previous match patterns.

There are following two methods for organising the associative memory based on bit slices:

Bit parallel organisation: In this organisation all bit slices which are not masked off, participate in the comparison process, i.e., all words are used in parallel.

Bit Serial Organisation: In this organisation, only one bit slice participate in the operation across all the words. The bit slice is selected through an extra logic and control unit. This organisation is slower in speed but requires lesser hardware as compared to bit parallel which is faster.

Types of Associative Processor

Based on the associative memory organisations, we can classify the associative processors into the following categories:

1) Fully Parallel Associative Processor: This processor adopts the bit parallel memory organisation. There are two type of this associative processor:

   Word Organized associative processor: In this processor one comparison logic is used with each bit cell of every word and the logical decision is achieved at the output of every word.

   Distributed associative processor: In this processor comparison logic is provided with each character cell of a fixed number of bits or with a group of character cells. This is less complex and therefore less expensive compared to word organized associative processor.

2) Bit Serial Associative Processor: When the associative processor adopts bit serial memory organization then it is called bit serial associative processor. Since only one bit slice is involved in the parallel operations, logic is very much reduced and therefore this processor is much less expensive than the fully parallel associative processor.

PEPE is an example of distributed associative processor which was designed as a special purpose computer for performing real time radar tracking in a missile environment. STARAN is an example of a bit serial associative processor which was designed for digital image processing. There is a high cost performance ratio of associative processors. Due to this reason these have not been commercialised and are limited to military applications.

MULTI-THREADED PROCESSORS

In unit 2, we have seen the use of distributed shared memory in parallel computer architecture. But the use of distributed shared memory has the problem of accessing the remote memory, which results in latency problems. This problem increases in case of large-scale multiprocessors like massively parallel processors (MPP).

For example, one processor in a multiprocessor system needs two memory loads of two variables from two remote processors as shown in *Figure 12*. The issuing processor will use these variables simultaneously in one operation. In case of large-scale MPP systems, the following two problems arise:

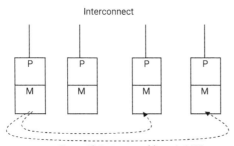

Figure 12: Latency problems in MPP

Remote-load Latency Problem: When one processor needs some remote loading of data from other nodes, then the processor has to wait for these two remote load operations. The longer the time taken in remote loading, the greater will be the latency and idle period of the issuing processor.

Synchronization Latency Problem: If two concurrent processes are performing remote loading, then it is not known by what time two processes will load, as the issuing processor needs two remote memory loads by two processes together for some operation. That means two concurrent processes return the results asynchronously and this causes the synchronization latency for the processor.

Concept of Multithreading: These problems increase in the design of large-scale multiprocessors such as MPP as discussed above. Therefore, a solution for optimizing these latency should be acquired at. The concept of *Multithreading* offers the solution to these problems. When the processor activities are multiplexed among many threads of execution, then problems are not occurring. In single threaded systems, only one thread of execution per process is present. But if we multiplex the activities of process among several threads, then the multithreading concept removes the latency problems.

In the above example, if multithreading is implemented, then one thread can be for issuing a remote load request from one variable and another thread can be for remote load for second variable and third thread can be for another operation for the processor and so on.

Multithreaded Architecture: It is clear now that if we provide many contexts to multiple threads, then processors with multiple contexts are called multithreaded systems. These systems are implemented in a manner similar to multitasking systems. A multithreaded processor will suspend the current context and switch to another. In this way, the processor will be busy most of the time and latency problems will also be optimized. Multithreaded architecture depends on the context switching time between the threads. The switching time should be very less as compared to latency time.

The processor utilization or its efficiency can be measured as:

$U = P / (P + I + S)$

where

P = useful processing time for which processor is busy I = Idle time when processor is waiting

S = Context switch time used for changing the active thread on the processor.

5

PERFORMANCE ANALYSIS OF PARALLEL COMPUTING

Introduction
Definitions
      Performance analysis
      Performance analysis techniques
      Performance analysis metrics
Efficiency
Speedup
Amdahl's Law
Gustafson Law
Gustafson-Barsis's Law
Superlinear Speedup and Efficiency
The Karp-Flatt Metric
The Isoefficiency Metric
Isoefficiency Relation
Cost and Scalability.

Introduction

The goal of all computer system users and designers is to get the highest performance at the lowest cost. Basic knowledge of performance evaluation terminology and technology is a must for computer professionals to evaluate their systems. Performance analysis is required at every stage of the life cycle of a computer system, starting from the design stage to manufacturing, sales, and upgrade. Designers do performance analysis when they want to compare a number of alternative designs and pick the best design, system administrators use performance analysis to choose a system from a set of possible systems for a certain application, and users need to know how well their systems are performing and if an upgrade is needed.

Performance analysis. The ideal performance of a computer system can be achieved if a perfect match between hardware capability and software behavior is reached.

Performance analysis techniques Three analysis techniques are used for performance analysis; these are analytical modeling, simulation, and measurement. To choose which one to use for the analysis of a system depends on certain considerations. The most important consideration is the stage in which the analysis is to be performed, measurement can't be performed unless the system already exists or at least a similar system does, if the proposed design is a new idea then only analytical modeling or simulation techniques can be used.

Analytical modeling. Used if the system is in the early design stages, and the results are needed soon. Provides insight into the underlying system, but it may not be precise due to simplification in modeling and mathematical equations.

Simulation. It is a useful technique for analysis. Simulation models provide easy ways to predict the performance of computer systems before they exist and it is used to validate the results of analytical modeling and measurement. Simulation provides snapshots of system behavior

Measurement. It can be used only if the system is available for measurement (postprototype) or at least other systems similar to the system under design exist. Its cost is high compared to the other two techniques because instruments of hardware and software are needed to perform measurements. It also takes a long time to monitor the system efficiently. The most important considerations that are used to choose one or more of these three techniques are illustrated in Figure 1 below.

Most important	Criterion	Analytical Modeling	Simulation	Measurement
	stage	Any	Any	postprototype
	Time required	Small	Medium	Varies
	Tools	Analysts	Computer Languages	Instruments
Figure	Accuracy Cost	Low small	Moderate Medium	Varies High

Performance metrics. Each performance study has different metrics that can be defined and used to evaluate that specific system under study, although these metrics are varied and different from one system to another, common metrics exist and are used in most general computer system evaluation. These most common metrics are introduced here.

Response time. It is the interval between a users request and the system response. In general the response time increases as the load increases, terms that are related to the response time are *turnaround* time and *reaction* time, turnaround time is defined as the time elapsed between submitting a job and the completion of its output, reaction time elapsed between submitting of a request and the beginning of its execution by the computer system. Stretch factor is the ratio of the response time at a particular load to that at a minimum load.

Throughput is defined as the rate (requests per unit time) at which the request can be serviced by the system, for CPUs the rate is measured in million instructions per second (MIPS) or million floating point instructions per second (Mflops), for networks the rate is measured in bits per second (bps) or packets per second, and for transaction systems it is measured in transactions per second (TPS). In general the throughput of a the system increases as the load initially increases, then after a certain load the throughput stops increasing and in some cases starts decreasing.

Speedup S(n). It is an indication of the degree of the speed gain in parallel computations. It is discussed in more detail later in this paper. There are three different speedup measures, asymptotic speedup, harmonic speedup, and Amdahl's speedup law, simply the speedup is defined as the ratio of the time taken by one processor to execute a program to the time taken by n processors to execute the same program.

$$S(n) = T(1)/T(n)$$

Parallel speedup is defined as the ratio of the time required to compute some function using a single processor (T_1) divided by the time required to compute it using P processors (T_P). That is: speedup = T_1/T_P. For example if it takes 10 seconds to run a program sequentially and 2 seconds to run it in parallel on some number of processors, P, then the speedup is 10/2=5 times.

System Efficiency *E(n)*. It is defined as the ratio of the maximum achievable throughput (usable capacity) to the maximum achievable capacity under ideal workload conditions. It is an indication of the actual degree of speedup performance achieved as compared with the maximum value for parallel processing, in other words it is the ratio of the performance of n-processor system to that of a single-processor system. The lowest efficiency corresponds to the case where the entire program code being executed sequentially on a single processor. The maximum efficiency corresponds to the case when all processors are fully utilized throughout the execution period. The minimum efficiency is the case where the entire program code being executed sequentially on a single processor as illustrated in figure 3.

Parallel efficiency measures how much use of the parallel processors we are making. For P processors, it is defined as: efficiency= 1/P x speedup= 1/P x T_1/T_P. For example, continuing with the same example, if P is 10 processors and the speedup is 5 times, then the parallel efficiency is 5/10=.5. In other words, on average, only half of the processors were used to gain the speedup and the other half were idle.

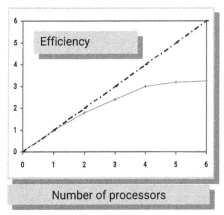

Figure: efficiency

$$\text{Efficiency} = \frac{\text{Speedup}}{\text{No\_processors}} = \frac{\text{Sequential ExecutionTime}}{\text{No\_processors X Parallel Execution Time}}$$

Amdahl's law

Amdahl's law states that in parallelization, if P is the proportion of a system or program that can be made parallel, and 1-P is the proportion that remains serial, then the maximum speedup that can be achieved using N number of processors is

$$= \frac{1}{(1-P)+(P/N)}.$$

If N tends to infinity then the maximum speedup tends to 1/(1-P).

Speedup is limited by the total time needed for the sequential (serial) part of the program. For 10 hours of computing, if we can parallelize 9 hours of computing and 1 hour cannot be parallelized, then our maximum speedup is limited to 10x.

The theory of multiprocessor computing shows that there is a mathematical limit on how fast a real parallelized program may go.
When a program runs on more than one CPU, its total run time should be less. But how much less? And what are the limits on the speedup?
Here, for example we have a system in which 40% operations are floating point. Suppose we enhance floating point unit such that it becomes 30 times faster. Now,we need to find overall speedup to the system. So, according to formula,
here,p=40/100=0.4 (we need to express p in proportion)
    s=30

Total Speedup =1/((1-0.4)+(0.4/30))
                =1/((0.6)+0.014)
                =1/(0.614)
                =1.62

Amdahl's law states that the maximum speedup possible in parallelizing an algorithm is limited by the sequential portion of the code. Given an algorithm which is P% parallel, Amdahl's law states that: MaximumSpeedup=1/(1- (P/100)). For example if 80% of a program is parallel, then the maximum speedup is 1/(1-0.8)=1/.2=5 times. If the program in question took 10 seconds to run serially, the best we could hope for in a parallel execution would be for it to take 2 seconds (10/5=2). This is because the serial 20% of the program cannot be sped up and it takes .2 x 10 seconds = 2 seconds even if the rest of the code is run perfectly in parallel on an infinite number of processors so it takes 0 seconds to execute.

Let us now look at how the maximum improvement can be calculated using Amdahl's law. For a given system, if the part that can be improved is 25% of the overall system and its performance can be doubled, then

$$S_{max} = \frac{1}{(1-0.25) + \frac{0.25}{2}} = 1.14$$

Let us suppose that for a different system, the part that can be improved is 75% of the overall system and its performance can be doubled, then

$$S_{max} = \frac{1}{(1 - 0.75) + \frac{0.75}{2}} = 1.6$$

The outcomes of analysis of Amdahl's law are:
To optimize the performance of parallel computers, modified compilers need to be developed which should aim to reduce the number of sequential operations pertaining to the fraction α.

The manufacturers of parallel computers were discouraged from manufacturing large-scale machines having millions of processors.

There is one major shortcoming identified in Amdahl's law. According to Amdahl's law, the workload or the problem size is always fixed and the number of sequential operations mainly remains same. That is, it assumes that the distribution of number of sequential operations and parallel operations always remains same.

Parallel Speedup and Amdahl's Law

The speedup gained from applying n CPUs, Speedup(n), is the ratio of the one-CPU execution time to the n-CPU parallel execution time: Speedup(n) = T(1)/T(n). If you measure the one-CPU execution time of a program at 100 seconds, and the program runs in 60 seconds with 2 CPUs, Speedup(2) = 100/60 = 1.67.

This number captures the improvement from adding hardware to the system. We expect T(n) to be less than T(1); if it is not, adding CPUs has made the program slower, and something is wrong! So Speedup(n) should be a number greater than 1.0, and the greater it is, the more pleased we are. Intuitively you might hope that the speedup would be equal to the number of CPUs --- twice as many CPUs, half the time --- but this ideal can quite never be achieved.
Normally, the number Speedup(n) must be less than n, reflecting the fact that not all parts of a program benefit from parallel execution. However, it is possible --- in rare situations --- for Speedup(n) to be larger than n. This is called a superlinear speedup --- the program has been speed up by more than the increase of CPUs.

There are always parts of a program that you cannot make parallel --- code that must run serially. The serial parts of the program cannot be speeded up by concurrency.

The mathematical statement of this idea is called Amdahl's law. Let p be the fraction of the program's code that can be made parallel (p is always a fraction less than 1.0.) The remaining (1-p) of the code must run serially. In practical cases, p ranges from 0.2 to 0.99.

The potential speedup for a program is proportional to p divided by the CPUs you can apply, plus the remaining serial part, (1-p):

Speedup(n) = $\frac{1}{(p/n)+(1-p)}$ (Amdahl's law: Speedup(n) given p)

The fraction p has a strong effect on the possible speedup, as shown in this graph:

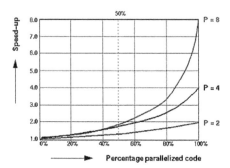

In particular, the more CPUs you have, the more benefit you get from increasing p. Using only 4 CPUs, you need only p = 0.6 to get half the ideal speedup. With 8 CPUs, you need p = 0.85 to get half the ideal speedup.

Predicting Execution Time with n CPUs

In some cases, the Speedup(2) = T(1)/T(2) is a value greater than 2, in other words, a superlinear speedup (described earlier). When this occurs, the formula in the preceding section returns a value of p greater than 1.0, clearly not useful. In this case you need to calculate p from two other more realistic timings, for example T(2) and T(3). The general formula for p is:

$$p = \frac{\text{Speedup(n) - Speedup(m)}}{(1 - 1/n)*\text{Speedup(n)} - (1 - 1/m)*\text{Speedup(m)}}$$

where n and m are the two processor counts whose speedups are known. You can use this calculated value of p to extrapolate the potential speedup with higher numbers of processors.

What Kinds of Problems Do We Solve with Amdahl's Law?
Recall how we defined performance of a system that has been sped up:

$$\text{Speedup} = \frac{\text{Execution time before improvement}}{\text{Execution time after improvement}}$$

There are three types of problems to be solved using the following Amdahl's Law equation:

$$\text{Speedup} = \frac{1}{(1 - \text{fraction enhanced}) + (\text{fraction enhanced/factor of improvement})}$$

Let Speedup be denoted by "S", fraction enhanced be denoted by "fE", and factor of improvement be denoted by "fI". Then we can write the above equation as

$$S = ((1 - fE) + (fE / fI))^{-1} .$$

The three problem types are as follows:

Determine S given fE and fI
Determine fI given S and fE

Determine fE given S and fl

Let us consider an example of each type of problem, as follows.

Problem Type 1 – Predict System Speedup
If we know fE and fl, then we use the Speedup equation (above) to determine S.

Example: Let a program have 40 percent of its code enhanced (so fE = 0.4) to run 2.3 times faster (so fl = 2.3). What is the overall system speedup S?

Step 1: Setup the equation: $S = ((1 - fE) + (fE / fl))^{-1}$
Step 2: Plug in values & solve $S = ((1 - 0.4) + (0.4 / 2.3))^{-1}$
             (0.6 + 0.174)-1 = 1 / 0.774
             1.292

Problem Type 2 – Predict Speedup of Fraction Enhanced
If we know fE and S, then we solve the Speedup equation (above) to determine fl , as follows:
Example: Let a program have 40 percent of its code enhanced (so fE = 0.4) to yield a system speedup 4.3 times faster (so S = 4.3). What is the factor of improvement fl of the portion enhanced?

Case #1:
Can we do this? In other words, let's determine if by enhancing 40 percent of the system, it is possible to make the system go 4.3 times faster ...

Step 1: Assume the limit, where fl = infinity, so $S = ((1 - fE) + (fE / fl))^{-1}$ ∥ $S = 1 / (1 - fE)$
Step 2: Plug in values & solve $S = ((1 - 0.4))^{-1} = 1 / 0.6 =$ **1.67** .
Step 3: So S = 1.67 is the **maximum possible speedup**, and we cannot achieve S = 4.3 !!

Case #2:
A different case: Let's determine if by enhancing 40 percent of the system, it is possible to make the system go 1.3 times faster ...
Step 1: Assume the limit, where fl = $S = ((1 - fE) + (fE / fl))^{-1}$ ∥ $S = 1 / (1 - fE)$
infinity, so
Step 2: Plug in values & solve $S = ((1 - 0.4))^{-1} = 1 / 0.6 =$ **1.67** .
Step 3: So S = 1.67 is the **maximum possible speedup**,
and we <u>can</u> achieve S = 1.3 !!
Step 4: Solve speedup equation for fl :   1/S [invert both sides]
= (1 - fE) + (fE / fl)
                         1/S - (1 - fE) = fE / fl   [subtract (1 - fE)]
                         (1/S - (1 - fE))^{-1} = fl / fE   [invert both sides]

                            fE · (1/S - (1 - fE))^{-1} = fl   [multiply by fE]
Step 5: Plug in values & solve: fl $= fE · (1/S - (1 - fE))^{-1}$
                         $= 0.4 · (1/1.3 - (1 - 0.4))^{-1}$
                         = 0.4 / (0.769 - 0.6) = **2.367**

Problem Type 3 – Predict Fraction of System to be Enhanced
If we know fl and S, then we solve the Speedup equation (above) to determine fE , as follows:
Example: Let a program have a portion fE of its code enhanced to run 4 times faster (so fl = 4), to yield a system speedup 3.3 times faster (so S = 3.3). What is the fraction enhanced (fE)?

Step 1: *Can this be done?*   Assuming fl = infinity, S = 3.3 = $((1 - fE))^{-1}$ so minimum fE = 0.697

Yes, this can be done for maximum fl, so let's solve the equation to determine <u>actual</u> fE

Step 2: Solve speedup equation for fE : $S = ((1 - fE) + (fE / fl))^{-1}$ [state the equation]

$3.3 = ((1 - fE) + (fE / 4))^{-1}$ [plug in values]

$(1 - fE) + fE/4 = 1/3.3 = $ [invert both sides] 0.303

$1 - 0.75fE = 0.303$ [regroup]

$0.75fE = 1 - 0.303 = 0.697$ [commutativity]

$fE = 0.697 / 0.75 = \textbf{0.929}$ [divide by 0.75]

Step 3: Check your work: $S = ((1 - fE) + (fE / fl))^{-1} = (0.071 + (0.929/4))^{-1} = 3.3$ [i]

Examples

If F is the fraction of a calculation that is sequential, and (1-F) is the fraction that can be parallelized, then the maximum speed-up that can be achieved by using P processors is 1/(F+(1-F)/P).

Examples
If 90% of a calculation can be parallelized (i.e. 10% is sequential) then the maximum speed-up which can be achieved on 5 processors is 1/(0.1+(1-0.1)/5) or roughly 3.6 (i.e. the program can theoritically run 3.6 times faster on five processors than on one)

Examples
If 90% of a calculation can be parallelized then the maximum speed-up on 10 processors is 1/(0.1+(1-0.1)/10) or 5.3 (i.e. investing twice as much hardware speeds the calculation up by about 50%).

If 90% of a calculation can be parallelized then the maximum speed-up on 20 processors is 1/(0.1+(1-0.1)/20) or 6.9 (i.e. doubling the hardware again speeds up the calculation by only 30%).

Examples
If 90% of a calculation can be parallelized then the maximum speed-up on 1000 processors is 1/(0.1+(1-0.1)/1000) or 9.9 (i.e. throwing an absurd amount of hardware at the calculation results in a maximum theoretical (i.e. actual results will be worse)

Essence
The point that Amdahl was trying to make was that using lots of parallel processors was not a viable way of achieving the sort of speed-ups that people were looking for. i.e. it was essentially an argument in support of investing effort in making single processor systems run faster.

Generalizations
The performance of any system is constrained by the speed or capacity of the slowest point.
The impact of an effort to improve the performance of a program is primarily constrained by the amount of time that the program spends in parts of the program not targeted by the effort

MAXIMUM THEORETICAL SPEED-UP

Law is a statement of the maximum theoretical speed-up you can ever hope to achieve. The actual speed-ups are always less than the speed-up predicted by Amdahl's Law

Why actual speed ups are always less?
Distributing work: to the parallel processors and collecting the results back together is extra work required in the parallel version which isn't required in the serial version.

Straggler problem: when the program is executing in the parallel parts of the code, it is unlikely that all of the processors will be computing all of the time as some of them will likely run out of work to do before others are finished their part of the parallel work.

Gustafson's Law

...speedup should be measured by scaling the problem to the number of processors, not by fixing the problem size.
— John Gustafson

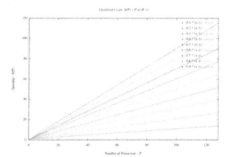

Figure. Gustafson's Law

Scaled speedup

Scaled speedup is the speedup that can be achieved by increasing the data size. This increase in data size is done to solve a given problem on multiple parallel processors. In other words, with larger number of parallel processors at our disposal, we can increase the data size of the same problem and achieve higher speedup. This is what is referred to as scaled speedup.

Gustafson argued that the sequential portion of a problem is not fixed and does not necessarily grow with problem size. For example, if the serial phase is only an initialization phase and the main calculations can run independently in parallel, then by increasing the problem size the sequential fraction can effectively be reduced to obtain a much larger speedup than that predicted by Amdahl's law.

Gustafson's Law says that it is possible to parallelize computations when they involve significantly large data sets. The Amdahl's law, which says that the maximum speedup that can be achieved in a given problem with serial fraction of work s, is 1/s, even when the number of processors increases to an infinite number. For example, if 5% of computation in a problem is serial, then the maximum achievable speedup is 20 regardless of the number of processors. This is not a very encouraging result.

Amdahl's law does not fully exploit the computing power that becomes available as the number of machines increases.

Gustafson's law addresses this limitation. Gustafson noted that problem sizes grow as computers become more powerful. As the problem size grows, the work required for the parallel part of the problem frequently grows much faster than the serial part. If this is true for a given application, then as the problem size grows the serial fraction decreases and speedup improves.

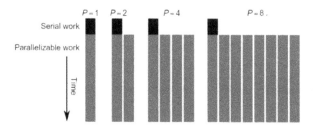

Figure: Gustafson-Barsis' Law; if the problem size increases with P while the serial portion grows slowly or remains fixed, speedup grows as processors are added.

Figure visualizes this using the assumption that the serial portion is constant while the parallel portion grows linearly with the problem size. On the left is the application running with one worker. As workers are added, the application solves bigger problems in the same time, not the same problem in less time. The serial portion still takes the same amount of time to perform, but diminishes as a fraction of the whole. Once the serial portion becomes insignificant, speedup grows practically at the same rate as the number of processors, thus achieving linear speedup.

It considers the effect of increasing the problem size. Gustafson reasoned that when a problem is ported onto a multiprocessor system, it is possible to consider larger problem sizes. In the same problem with a larger number of data values takes the same time. The law proposes that programmers tend to set the size of problems to use the available equipment to solve problems within a practical fixed time. Larger problems can be solved in the same time if faster, i.e. more parallel equipment is available. Therefore, it should be possible to achieve high speedup if we scale the problem size.

Example:

    s (serial fraction of work) = 5%
    p (number of processors) = 20
    speedup (Amdahl's Law) = 10.26
    scaled speedup (Gustafson's Law) = 19.05

Derivation of Gustafson's Law

If p is the number of processors, s is the amount of time spent (by a serial processor) on serial parts of a program and 1-s is the amount of time spent (by a serial processor) on parts of the program that can be done in parallel, then **Amdahl's law** says that speedup is given by:

$$\frac{s + (1 - s)}{s + \dfrac{(1 - s)}{p}} = \frac{1}{s + \dfrac{(1 - s)}{p}}$$

Let us consider a bigger problem size of measure n.

The execution of the program on a parallel computer is decomposed into:

$$s + (1 - s) = 1$$

where a is the sequential fraction, 1-s is the parallel fraction, ignoring overhead for now, and p is the number of processors working in parallel during the parallel stage.

The relative time for sequential processing would be $s + p \ (1 - s)$, where p is the number of processors in the parallel case.

Scaled Speedup is therefore: $p + (1-p)s$

where s: = s(n) is the sequential fraction.

Using this formula with s = 0.5 and 7 processors, we get a speedup of S = 7 + (-6).3 = 7-3 = 4.
Using Amdahl's Law (S = 1 / (s + (1-s)/N)), we get a speedup of S= 1 / (.5 + ((1- .5)/7) = 1.75 It is easy to see that this is a much more optimistic outlook than that of Amdahl's Law.

Q1. An application running on 10 processors spends 3% of its time in serial code. What is the scaled speedup of the application?

$$= 10 + (1 - 10)(0.03) = 10 - 0.27 = 9.73$$

Q2. What is the maximum fraction of a program's parallel execution time that can be spent in serial code if it is to achieve a scaled speedup of 7 on 8 processors?

$$7 = 8 + (1 - 8)s \Rightarrow s \approx 0.14$$

It is thus much easier to achieve efficient parallel performance than is implied by Amdahl's paradigm. The two approaches, fixed-sized and scaled-sized, are contrasted and summarized in Figure 2a and b.

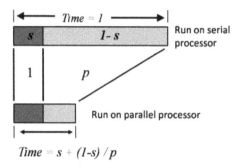

Figure a. Fixed-Size Model: Speedup = 1 / (s + (1-s) / p)

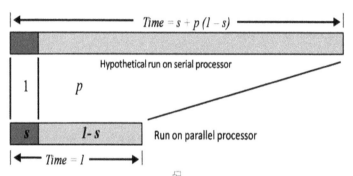

Figure b. Scaled-Size Model: Speedup = s + p (1-s)

The Gustafson-Barsis law states that speedup tends to increase with problem size (since the fraction of time spent executing serial code goes down). Gustafason-Barsis' law is thus a measure of what is known as "scaled speedup" (scaled by the number of processors used on a problem) and it can be stated as: MaximumScaledSpeedup=p+(1-p)s, where p is the number of processors and s is the fraction of total execution time spent in serial code. This law tells us that attainable speedup is often related to problem size not just the number of processors used. In essence Amdahl's law assumes that the percentage of serial code is independent of problem size. This is not necessarily true. (E.g. consider overhead for managing the parallelism: synchronization, etc.). Thus, in some sense, Gustafon-Barsis' law generalizes Amdahl's law.

Amdahl versus Gustafson Barsis

Gustafson's reference point is the available equipment, while Amdahl's reference point is the fixed problem size.

Amdahl's law encourages sticking with serial processing as long as possible, while Gustafson's law encourages parallelizing wherever possible.

Amdahl's Law (which posits that speedup is limited by the non-parallelizable serial portion of the work) and Gustafson-Barsis' Law (which posits that adding processors allows an application to solve bigger problems in the same time).

Superlinear speedup

Not too long ago, the parallel time to solve a given problem using p processors was believed to be no greater than p. However, people then observed that in some computations the speedup was greater than p. When the speedup is higher than p, it is called super-linear speedup. One thing that could hinder the chances of achieving **super-linear speedup** is the cost involved in inter-process communication during parallel computation. This is not a concern in serial computation. However, super-linear speedup can be achieved by utilizing the resources very efficiently.

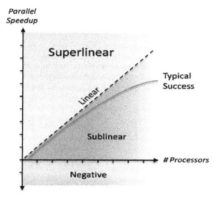

Figure: Super-linear speedup

Reasons for super-linear speedup

Let us look at the reasons for super-linear speedup. The data set of a given problem could be much larger than the cache size when the problem is executed serially. In **parallel computation**, however, the data set has enough space in each cache that is available. In problems that involve searching a data structure, multiple searches can be executed at the same time. This reduces the termination time. Another reason is the efficient utilization of resources by **multiprocessors**.

Super-linearity on a large machine

So far we have looked at leveraging the super-linearity that can arise naturally in parallel computation. Now let us think how else we could achieve super-linear speedup. We could use more parallelism on the same machine. To speed up computational work we can increase the number of cores that we use. However, using more cores will only give us linear speedup.

When you run a program with less parallelism and another with more parallelism on the same modern desktop or server hardware, the one with more parallelism literally runs on a bigger machine — a disproportionately larger share of the available hardware. This happens because the one with more parallelism can use not only additional cores, but additional hardware resources attached to those cores that would not otherwise be available to the program. In particular, using more cores also means getting access to more *cache* and/or more memory.

Let us take a look at Figure to see why this is so. This figure shows a simplified block diagram of the cores and caches on two modern commodity CPUs: the current *Intel "Kentsfield" processor*, and the upcoming *AMD "Barcelona" processor*, respectively. The interesting feature in both chips is that each core has access to cache memory that is not available to some or all of the other cores. In the Kentsfield processor, each pair of cores shares a private *L2 cache*; in the Barcelona chip, each core has its own private L2 cache.

In both cases, no core by itself has access to all the available L2 cache, and that means that code running on just one core is limited, not only to the one core, but also to just a fraction of the available cache. For code whose performance is memory bound, the amount of available cache can make a significant difference.

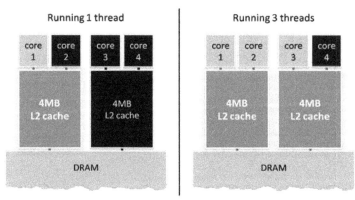

Figure . Intel Kentsfield core and cache utilization: 1 thread versus 3 threads

Example:

Suppose we have an 8 processor machine, each processor has a 1MB cache and each computation uses 6MB of data.

On a single processor the computation will be doing a lot of data movement between CPU, cache and RAM.

On 8 processors the computation will only have to move data between CPU and cache.
This way super-linear speedup can be achieved.

Controversy

Talk of super-linear speedup always sparks some controversy. Since super-linear speedup is not possible in theory, some non-orthodox practices could be thought of being the cause for achieving super-linear speedup. This is true especially with regard to the traditional research community. Hence, reporting super-linear speedup is controversial.

Karp–Flatt metric

The **Karp–Flatt metric** is a measure of *parallelization* of code in *parallel computation*. This metrices is an indication of the extent to which a particular computer code is parallelized. It was proposed by Alan H. Karp and Horace P. Flatt in 1990.

Amdahl's Law and Gustafson-Barsis' Law ignore processor communication and synchronization overhead $K(n,p)$. They can overestimate speedup or scaled speedup.

Given a parallel computation exhibiting *speedup* S on p processors, where $p > 1$, the experimentally determined *serial fraction* e is defined to be the Karp–Flatt Metric is:

$$e = \frac{1/S - 1/p}{1 - 1/p}$$

The less the value of e the better the parallelization.

There are many ways to measure the performance of a *parallel algorithm* running on a parallel processor. The Karp–Flatt metric defines a metric which reveals aspects of the performance that are not easily discerned from other metrics. A pseudo-"derivation" of sorts follows from *Amdahl's Law*, which can be written as:

$T(p) = T(s) + (T(p) / p)$

Where:

- $T(p)$ is the total time taken for code execution in a p-processor system.

- Ts is the time taken for the serial part of the code to run.

- Tp is the time taken for the parallel part of the code to run in one processor.

- p is the number of processors.

In terms of the *speedup*

$$1/S = e + (1 - e/p)$$

Solving for the serial fraction, we get the Karp–Flatt metric as above. Experimentally Determined Serial Fraction

1. Takes into account parallel overhead
2. Detects other sources of overhead or inefficiency ignored in speedup model
   - Process startup time
   - Process synchronization time
   - Imbalanced workload
   - Architectural overhead

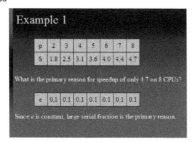

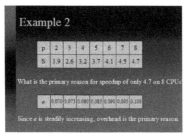

The Isoefficiency Metric of Scalability

For a given problem size, as we increase the number of processing elements, the overall efficiency of the parallel system goes down. This phenomenon is common to all parallel systems. The isoefficiency metric is specifically used to measure the scalability of a parallel algorithm.

In many cases, the efficiency of a parallel system increases if the problem size is increased while keeping the number of processing elements constant.

These two phenomena are illustrated in **Figure (a)** and **(b)**, respectively. Following from these two observations, we define a scalable parallel system as one in which the efficiency can be kept constant as the number of processing elements is increased, provided that the problem size is also increased. It is useful to determine the rate at which the problem size must increase with respect to the number of processing elements to keep the efficiency fixed. For different parallel systems, the problem size must increase at different rates in order to maintain a fixed efficiency as the number of processing elements is increased. This rate determines the degree of scalability of the parallel system. As we shall show, a lower rate is more desirable than a higher growth rate in problem size. Let us now investigate metrics for quantitatively determining the degree of scalability of a parallel system. However, before we do that, we must define the notion of **problem size** precisely.

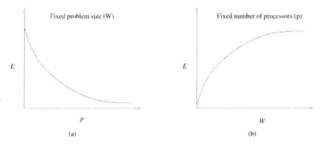

Figure: Variation of efficiency: (a) as the number of processing elements is increased for a given problem size; and (b) as the problem size is increased for a given number of processing elements. The phenomenon illustrated in graph (b) is not common to all parallel systems.

Problem Size When analyzing parallel systems, we frequently encounter the notion of the size of the problem being solved. Thus far, we have used the term **problem size** informally, without giving a precise definition. A naive way to express problem size is as a parameter of the input size; for instance, n in case of a matrix operation involving $n \times n$ matrices. A drawback of this definition is that the interpretation of problem size changes from one problem to another. For example, doubling the input size results in an eight-fold increase in the execution time for matrix multiplication and a four-fold increase for matrix addition (assuming that the conventional $Q(n^3)$ algorithm is the best matrix multiplication algorithm, and disregarding more complicated algorithms with better asymptotic complexities).

A consistent definition of the size or the magnitude of the problem should be such that, regardless of the problem, doubling the problem size always means performing twice the amount of computation. Therefore, we choose to express problem size in terms of the total number of basic operations required to solve the problem. By this definition, the problem size is $Q(n^3)$ for $n \times n$ matrix multiplication (assuming the conventional algorithm) and $Q(n^2)$ for $n \times n$ matrix addition.

The symbol we use to denote problem size is W.

In the remainder of this chapter, we assume that it takes unit time to perform one basic computation step of an algorithm. This assumption does not impact the analysis of any parallel system because the other hardware-related constants, such as message startup time, per-word transfer time, and per-hop time, can be normalized with respect to the time taken by a basic computation step. With this assumption, the problem size W is equal to the serial runtime T_S of the fastest known algorithm to solve the problem on a sequential computer.

The Isoefficiency Function

Parallel execution time can be expressed as a function of problem size, overhead function, and the number of processing elements. We can write parallel runtime as:

Equation 5.10

$$T_P = \frac{W + T_o(W, p)}{p}$$

The resulting expression for speedup is

Equation 5.11

$$S = \frac{W}{T_P}$$
$$= \frac{Wp}{W + T_o(W, p)}.$$

Finally, we write the expression for efficiency as

Equation 5.12

$$E = \frac{S}{p}$$
$$= \frac{W}{W + T_o(W, p)}$$
$$= \frac{1}{1 + T_o(W, p)/W}.$$

In **Equation 5.12**, if the problem size is kept constant and p is increased, the efficiency decreases because the total overhead T_o increases with p. If W is increased keeping the number of processing elements fixed, then for scalable parallel systems, the efficiency increases. This is because T_o grows slower than $Q(W)$ for a fixed p. For these parallel systems, efficiency can be maintained at a desired value (between 0 and 1) for increasing p, provided W is also increased.

For different parallel systems, W must be increased at different rates with respect to p in order to maintain a fixed efficiency. For instance, in some cases, W might need to grow as an exponential function of p to keep the efficiency from dropping as p increases. Such parallel systems are poorly scalable. The reason is that on these parallel systems it is difficult to obtain good speedups for a large number of processing elements unless the problem size is enormous. On the other hand, if W needs to grow only linearly with respect to p, then the parallel system is highly scalable. That is because it can easily deliver speedups proportional to the number of processing elements for reasonable problem sizes.

For scalable parallel systems, efficiency can be maintained at a fixed value (between 0 and 1) if the ratio T_o/W in **Equation 5.12** is maintained at a constant value. For a desired value E of efficiency,

Equation 5.13

$$E = \frac{1}{1 + T_o(W, p)/W},$$

$$\frac{T_o(W, p)}{W} = \frac{1 - E}{E},$$

$$W = \frac{E}{1 - E} T_o(W, p).$$

Let $K = E/(1 - E)$ be a constant depending on the efficiency to be maintained. Since T_o is a function of W and p, **Equation 5.13** can be rewritten as

Equation 5.14

$$W = KT_o(W, p).$$

From **Equation 5.14**, the problem size W can usually be obtained as a function of p by algebraic manipulations. This function dictates the growth rate of W required to keep the efficiency fixed as p increases. We call this function the *isoefficiency function* of the parallel system. The isoefficiency function determines the ease with which a parallel system can maintain a constant efficiency and hence achieve speedups increasing in proportion to the number of processing elements. A small isoefficiency function means that small increments in the problem size are sufficient for the efficient utilization of an increasing number of processing elements, indicating that the parallel system is highly scalable. However, a large isoefficiency function indicates a poorly scalable parallel system. The isoefficiency function does not exist for unscalable parallel systems, because in such systems the efficiency cannot be kept at any constant value as p increases, no matter how fast the problem size is increased.

Cost

We define the **cost** of solving a problem on a parallel system as the product of parallel runtime and the number of processing elements used. Cost reflects the sum of the time that each processing element spends solving the problem. Efficiency can also be expressed as the ratio of the execution time of the fastest known sequential algorithm for solving a problem to the cost of solving the same problem on p processing elements.

The cost of solving a problem on a single processing element is the execution time of the fastest known sequential algorithm. A parallel system is said to be **cost-optimal** if the cost of solving a problem on a parallel computer has the same asymptotic growth (in Q terms) as a function of the input size as the fastest-known sequential algorithm on a single processing element. Since efficiency is the ratio of sequential cost to parallel cost, a cost-optimal parallel system has an efficiency of Q(1).
Cost is sometimes referred to as **work** or **processor-time product**, and a cost-optimal system is also known as a pT_P-optimal system.

Example: Cost of adding n numbers on n processing elements

Consider the problem of adding n numbers by using n processing elements. Initially, each processing element is assigned one of the numbers to be added and, at the end of the computation, one of the processing elements stores the sum of all the numbers. Assuming that n is a power of two, we can perform this operation in log n steps by propagating partial sums up a logical binary tree of processing elements. **Figure** illustrates the procedure for $n = 16$. The processing elements are labeled from 0 to 15. Similarly, the 16 numbers to be added are labeled from 0 to 15. The sum of the numbers with consecutive labels from i to j is denoted by Σ_i^j.

Figure: Computing the globalsum of 16 partial sums using 16 processing elements. Σ_i^j denotes the sum of numbers with consecutive labels from i to j.

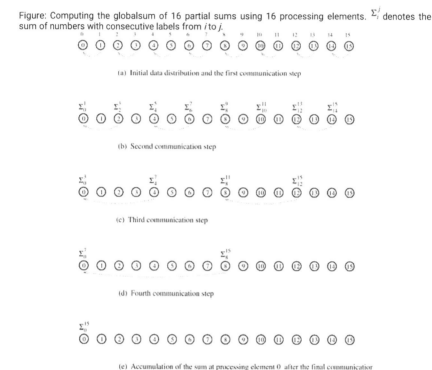

(a) Initial data distribution and the first communication step

(b) Second communication step

(c) Third communication step

(d) Fourth communication step

(e) Accumulation of the sum at processing element 0 after the final communication

The algorithm given in **Example** for adding n numbers on n processing elements has a processor-time product of Q($n \log n$). Since the serial runtime of this operation is Q(n), the

Scalability of Parallel Systems

Very often, programs are designed and tested for smaller problems on fewer processing elements. However, the real problems these programs are intended to solve are much larger, and the machines contain larger number of processing elements. Whereas code development is simplified by using scaled-down versions of the machine and the problem, their performance and correctness (of programs) is much more difficult to establish based on scaled-down systems. In this section, we will investigate techniques for evaluating the scalability of parallel programs using analytical tools.

Example: Why is performance extrapolation so difficult?
Consider three parallel algorithms for computing an n-point Fast Fourier Transform (FFT) on 64 processing elements. **Figure** illustrates speedup as the value of n is increased to 18 K. Keeping the number of processing elements constant, at smaller values of n, one would infer from observed speedups that binary exchange and 3-D transpose algorithms are the best.

However, as the problem is scaled up to 18 K points or more, it is evident from **Figure** that the 2-D transpose algorithm yields best speedup.

Figure 5.7. A comparison of the speedups obtained by the binary-exchange, 2-D transpose and 3-D transpose algorithms on 64 processing elements with $t_c = 2$, $t_w = 4$, $t_s = 25$, and $t_h = 2$

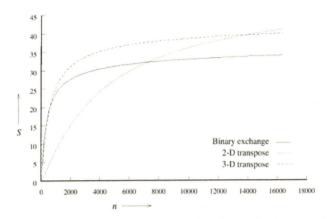

Similar results can be shown relating to the variation in number of processing elements as the problem size is held constant. Unfortunately, such parallel performance traces are the norm as opposed to the exception, making performance prediction based on limited observed data very difficult.

Scaling Characteristics of Parallel Programs

The efficiency of a parallel program can be written as:

$$E = \frac{S}{p} = \frac{T_S}{pT_P}$$

Using the expression for parallel overhead (**Equation 5.1**), we can rewrite this expression as

Equation 5.15

$$E = \frac{1}{1 + \frac{T_o}{T_S}}.$$

The total overhead function T_o is an increasing function of p. This is because every program must contain some serial component. If this serial component of the program takes time t_{serial}, then during this time all the other processing elements must be idle. This corresponds to a total overhead function of $(p - 1) \times t_{serial}$. Therefore, the total overhead function T_o grows at least linearly with p. In addition, due to communication, idling, and excess computation, this function may grow superlinearly in the number of processing elements.

Equation 5.15 gives us several interesting insights into the scaling of parallel programs. First, for a given problem size (i.e. the value of T_S remains constant), as we increase the number of processing elements, T_o increases. In such a scenario, it is clear from **Equation 5.15** that the overall efficiency of the parallel program goes down. This characteristic of decreasing efficiency with increasing number of processing elements for a given problem size is common to all parallel programs.

6

PARALLEL COMPUTATIONAL MODEL

PRAM
CRCW
CREW
EREW,
Simulating CRCW on CREW & SREW
PRAM algorithms
P-Complete problems.

A parallel computational model is one in which each program instruction is executed simultaneously on multiple processors in order to get the results faster. Using multi-cores in processors is an example of parallel computing. It is by using parallel processing that super computers are getting faster and faster.

Parallel Random-Access Machines

Sheperdson and Sturgis (1963) modeled the conventional Uniprocessor computers as random-access-machines (RAM). Fortune and Wyllie (1978) developed a parallel random-access-machine (PRAM) model for modeling an idealized parallel computer with zero memory access overhead and synchronization.

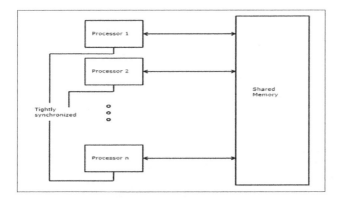

Parallel Random Access Machines (PRAM) is a model, which is considered for most of the parallel algorithms. Here, multiple processors are attached to a single block of memory. A PRAM model contains –

- A set of similar type of processors.
- All the processors share a common memory unit. Processors can communicate among themselves through the shared memory only.
- A memory access unit (MAU) connects the processors with the single shared memory.

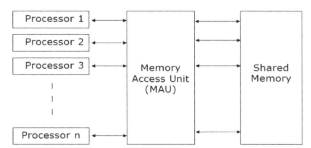

Here, **n** number of processors can perform independent operations on **n** number of data in a particular unit of time. This may result in simultaneous access of same memory location by different processors. To solve this problem, the following constraints have been enforced on PRAM model –

Exclusive Read Exclusive Write (EREW) – Here no two processors are allowed to read from or write to the same memory location at the same time.

Exclusive Read Concurrent Write (ERCW) – Here no two processors are allowed to read from the same memory location at the same time, but are allowed to write to the same memory location at the same time.

Concurrent Read Exclusive Write (CREW) – Here all the processors are allowed to read from the same memory location at the same time, but are not allowed to write to the same memory location at the same time.

Concurrent Read Concurrent Write (CRCW) – All the processors are allowed to read from or write to the same memory location at the same time.

There are many methods to implement the PRAM model, but the most prominent ones are

- Shared memory model
- Message passing model
- Data parallel model

Shared Memory Model

Shared memory emphasizes on **control parallelism** than on **data parallelism**. In the shared memory model, multiple processes execute on different processors independently, but they share a common memory space. Due to any processor activity, if there is any change in any memory location, it is visible to the rest of the processors.

As multiple processors access the same memory location, it may happen that at any particular point of time, more than one processor is accessing the same memory location. Suppose one is reading that location and the other is writing on that location. It may create confusion. To avoid this, some control mechanism, like **lock / semaphore,** is implemented to ensure mutual exclusion.

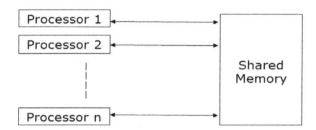

Shared memory programming has been implemented in the following –

Thread libraries – The thread library allows multiple threads of control that run concurrently in the same memory location. Thread library provides an interface that supports multithreading through a library of subroutine. It contains subroutines for

o   Creating and destroying threads
o   Scheduling execution of thread
o   passing data and message between threads
o   saving and restoring thread contexts

Examples of thread libraries include – SolarisTM threads for Solaris, POSIX threads as implemented in Linux, Win32 threads available in Windows NT and Windows 2000, and JavaTM threads as part of the standard JavaTM Development Kit (JDK).

Distributed Shared Memory (DSM) Systems – DSM systems create an abstraction of shared memory on loosely coupled architecture in order to implement shared memory programming without hardware support. They implement standard libraries and use the advanced user-level memory management features present in modern operating systems. Examples include Tread Marks System, Munin, IVY, Shasta, Brazos, and Cashmere.

Program Annotation Packages – This is implemented on the architectures having uniform memory access characteristics. The most notable example of program annotation packages is OpenMP. OpenMP implements functional parallelism. It mainly focuses on parallelization of loops.
The concept of shared memory provides a low-level control of shared memory system, but it tends to be tedious and erroneous. It is more applicable for system programming than application programming.
Merits of Shared Memory Programming

▪   Global address space gives a user-friendly programming approach to memory.
▪   Due to the closeness of memory to CPU, data sharing among processes is fast and uniform.
▪   There is no need to specify distinctly the communication of data among processes.
▪   Process-communication overhead is negligible.
▪   It is very easy to learn.

Demerits of Shared Memory Programming

- It is not portable.
- Managing data locality is very difficult.

Message Passing Model

Message passing is the most commonly used parallel programming approach in distributed memory systems. Here, the programmer has to determine the parallelism. In this model, all the processors have their own local memory unit and they exchange data through a communication network.

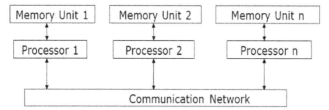

Processors use message-passing libraries for communication among themselves. Along with the data being sent, the message contains the following components –

- The address of the processor from which the message is being sent;
- Starting address of the memory location of the data in the sending processor;
- Data type of the sending data;
- Data size of the sending data;
- The address of the processor to which the message is being sent;
- Starting address of the memory location for the data in the receiving processor.

Processors can communicate with each other by any of the following methods –

- Point-to-Point Communication
- Collective Communication
- Message Passing Interface

Point-to-Point Communication

Point-to-point communication is the simplest form of message passing. Here, a message can be sent from the sending processor to a receiving processor by any of the following transfer modes –

Synchronous mode – The next message is sent only after the receiving a confirmation that its previous message has been delivered, to maintain the sequence of the message.
Asynchronous mode – To send the next message, receipt of the confirmation of the delivery of the previous message is not required.

Collective Communication

Collective communication involves more than two processors for message passing. Following modes allow collective communications –

Barrier – Barrier mode is possible if all the processors included in the communications run a particular bock (known as **barrier block**) for message passing.

Broadcast – Broadcasting is of two types –
>**One-to-all** – Here, one processor with a single operation sends same message to all other processors.
>**All-to-all** – Here, all processors send message to all other processors.

Messages broadcasted may be of three types –

>**1. Personalized** – Unique messages are sent to all other destination processors.
>**2. Non-personalized** – All the destination processors receive the same message.
>**3. Reduction** – In reduction broadcasting, one processor of the group collects all the messages from all other processors in the group and combine them to a single message which all other processors in the group can access.

Merits of Message Passing

- Provides low-level control of parallelism;
- It is portable;
- Less error prone;
- Less overhead in parallel synchronization and data distribution.

Demerits of Message Passing

As compared to parallel shared-memory code, message-passing code generally needs more software overhead.

Message Passing Libraries

There are many message-passing libraries. Here, we will discuss two of the most-used message-passing libraries –
- Message Passing Interface (MPI)
- Parallel Virtual Machine (PVM)

MESSAGE PASSING INTERFACE (MPI)

It is a universal standard to provide communication among all the concurrent processes in a distributed memory system. Most of the commonly used parallel computing platforms provide at least one implementation of message passing interface. It has been implemented as the collection of predefined functions called **library** and can be called from languages such as C, C++, Fortran, etc. MPIs are both fast and portable as compared to the other message passing libraries.

Merits of Message Passing Interface

Runs only on shared memory architectures or distributed memory architectures;
Each processors has its own local variables;
As compared to large shared memory computers, distributed memory computers are less expensive.

Demerits of Message Passing Interface

More programming changes are required for parallel algorithm;
Sometimes difficult to debug; and

Does not perform well in the communication network between the nodes.

Simulating Multiple Accesses on an EREW PRAM

The EREWPRAM model is considered the most restrictive among the four subclasses discussed in the previous section. Only one processor can read from or write to a given memory location at any time. An algorithm designed for such a model must not rely on having multiple processors access the same memory location simultaneously in order to improve its performance. Obviously, an algorithm designed for an EREW PRAM can run on a CRCWPRAM. The algorithm simply will not use the concurrent access features in the CRCW PRAM. However, the contrary is not true, an algorithm designed for CRCW cannot run on an EREW PRAM.

Is it possible to simulate concurrent access in the EREW model? The answer is yes. In general, any algorithm designed to run on a given model can be simulated on a more restrictive model at the price of more time and/or memory requirements. Clearly, the EREW PRAM model is the most restrictive among the four PRAM subclasses. Hence, it is possible to simulate the concurrent read and write operations on an EREW PRAM. In what follows, we show that this simulation can be done at the price of $O(\log p)$ time and $O(p)$ memory, where p is the number of processors, using a broadcasting procedure.

Suppose that a memory location x is needed by all processors at a given time in a PRAM. Concurrent read by all processors can be performed in the CREW and CRCW cases in constant time. In the EREW case, the following broadcasting mechanism can be followed:

1. P1 reads x and makes it known to P2.
2. P1 and P2 make x known to P3 and P4, respectively, in parallel.
3. P1, P2, P3, and P4 make x known to P5, P6, P7, and P8, respectively, in parallel.
4. These eight processors will make x known to another eight processors, and so on.

In order to represent this algorithm in PRAM, an array L of size p is used as a working space in the shared memory to distribute the contents of x to all processors. Initially P1 will read x in its private memory and writes it into L[1]. Processor P2, will read x from L[1] into its private memory and write it into L[2]. Simultaneously, P3 and P4 read x from L[1] and L[2], respectively, then write them into L[3] and L[4], respectively. Processors P5 , P6 , P7 , and P8 will then simultaneously read L[1], L[2], L[3], and L[4], respectively, in parallel and write them into L[5], L[6], L[7], and L[8], respectively. This process will continue until eventually all the processors have read x. Figure 6.2 illustrates the idea of Algorithm Broadcast_EREW, when p = 8.

```
Algorithm Broadcast_EREW
Processor P₁
   y (in P₁'s private memory) ← x
   L[1] ← y
for i=0 to log p - 1 do
   forall Pⱼ, where 2ⁱ + 1 ≤ j ≤ 2^{i+1} do in parallel
      y (in Pⱼ's private memory) ← L[j - 2ⁱ]
      L[j] ← y
   endfor
endfor
```

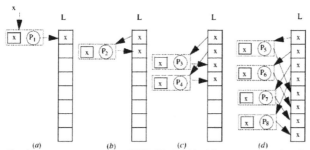

Figure: Simulating concurrent read on EREW PRAM with eight processors using algorithm broadcast_EREW.

Since the number of processors having read x doubles in each iteration, the procedure terminates in O(log p) time. The array L is the price paid in terms of memory, which is O(p).

Analysis of Parallel Algorithms

The complexity of a sequential algorithm is generally determined by its time and space complexity. The time complexity of an algorithm refers to its execution time as a function of the problem's size. Similarly, the space complexity refers to the amount of memory required by the algorithm as a function of the size of the problem. The time complexity has been known to be the most important measure of the performance of algorithms. An algorithm whose time complexity is bounded by a polynomial is called a polynomial–time algorithm. An algorithm is considered to be efficient if it runs in polynomial time. Inefficient algorithms are those that require a search of the whole enumerated space and have an exponential time complexity.

For parallel algorithms, the time complexity remains an important measure of performance. Additionally, the number of processors plays a major role in determining the complexity of a parallel algorithm. In general, we say that the performance of a parallel algorithm is expressed in terms of how fast it is, and how many resources it uses when it runs. These criteria can be measured quantitatively as follows:

    1. Run time, which is defined as the time spent during the execution of the algorithm.
    2. Number of processors the algorithm uses to solve a problem.
    3. The cost of the parallel algorithm, which is the product of the run time and the number of processors.

The run time of a parallel algorithm is the length of the time period between the time the first processor to begin execution starts and the time the last processor to finish execution terminates. However, since the analysis of algorithms is normally conducted before the algorithm is even implemented on an actual computer, the run time is usually obtained by counting the number of steps in the algorithm. The cost of a parallel algorithm is basically the total number of steps executed collectively by all processors. If the cost of an algorithm is C, the algorithm can be converted into a sequential one that runs in O(C) time on one processor. A parallel algorithm is said to be cost optimal if its cost matches the lower bound on the number of sequential operations to solve a given problem within a constant factor. It follows that a parallel algorithm is not cost optimal if there exists a sequential algorithm whose run time is smaller than the cost of the parallel algorithm.

It may be possible to speed up the execution of a cost-optimal PRAM algorithm by increasing the number of processors. However, we should be careful because using more processors may increase the cost of the parallel algorithm. Similarly, a PRAM algorithm may use fewer processors in order to reduce the cost. In this case the execution may be slowed down and offset the decrease in the number of processors. Therefore, using fewer processors requires that we make them work more efficiently. Further details on the relationship between the run time, number of processors, and optimal cost can be found in Brent (1974).

In order to design efficient parallel algorithms, one must consider the following general rules. The number of processors must be bounded by the size of the problem. The parallel run time must be significantly smaller than the execution time of the best sequential algorithm. The cost of the algorithm is optimal.

The NC-Class and P-Completeness

In the theory of sequential algorithms, we distinguish between tractable and intractable problems by categorizing them into different classes. For those who are not familiar with these classes, we define them in simple terms. A problem belongs to class P if a solution of the problem can be obtained by a polynomial-time algorithm.

A problem belongs to class NP if the correctness of a solution for the problem can be verified by a polynomial-time algorithm. Clearly, every problem in P will also be in NP, or $P \subseteq NP$. It remain an open problem whether $P \subset NP$ or $P = NP$. However, it is not likely that $P = NP$ since this would imply that solving a problem is as easy as verifying whether a given solution to the problem is correct. A problem is in the class NP-hard if it is as hard as any problem in NP. In other words, every NP problem is polynomial-time reducible to any NP-hard problem. The existence of a polynomial-time algorithm for an NP-hard problem implies the existence of polynomial solutions for every problem in NP. Finally, NP-complete problems are the NP-hard problems that are also in NP.

The NP-complete problems are the problems that are strongly suspected to be computationally intractable. There is a host of important problems that are roughly equivalent in complexity and form the class of NP-complete problems. This class includes many classical problems in combinatorics, graph theory, and computer science such as the traveling salesman problem, the Hamilton circuit problem, and integer programming.

The best known algorithms for these problems could take exponential time on some inputs. The exact complexity of these NP-complete problems has yet to be determined and it remains the foremost open problem in theoretical computer science. Either all these problems have polynomial-time solutions, or none of them does.

Similarly, in the world of parallel computation, we should be able to classify problems according to their use of the resources: time and processors. Let us define the class of the well-parallelizable problems, called NC, as the class of problem that have efficient parallel solutions. It is the class of problems that are solvable in time bounded by a polynomial in the log of the input size using a number of processors bounded by a polynomial in the input size. The time bound is sometimes referred to as *polylogarithmic* because it is polynomial in the log of the input size. In other words, the problems that can be solved by parallel algorithms that take polylogarithmic time using a polynomial number of processors, are said to belong to the class NC. The problems in the class NC are regarded as having efficient parallel solutions.

The question now is: what is the relation between NC and P? It remain an open question whether $NC \subset P$ or $NC = P$. It appears that some problems in P cannot be solved in polylogarithmic time using a polynomial number of processors. Thus, it is not likely that $NC = P$.

We finally discuss the P-complete problems. A problem is in the class P-complete if it is as hard to parallelize as any problem in P. In other words, every P problem is polylogarithmic-time reducible to any P-complete problem using a polynomial number of processors. Also, the existence of a polylogarithmic -time algorithm for a P-complete problem implies the existence of polylogarithmic solutions for every problem in P using a polynomial number of processors. In other words, a P-complete problem is the problem that is solvable sequentially in polynomial time, but does not lie in the class NC unless every problem solvable in sequential polynomial time lies in NC. Among examples of P-complete problems are a depth-first search of an arbitrary graph, the maximum-flow problem, and the circuit value problem. The relationships between all these classes are illustrated in Figure , if we assume that $P \subset NP$ and $NC \subset P$.

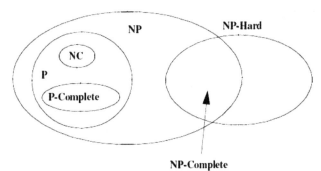

NP-Complete

Figure: The relationships among P, NP, NP-complete, NP-hard, NC, and P-complete($P \subset NP$ and $NC \subset P$).

7

INTRODUCTION TO PARALLEL ALGORITHMS

PVM
MPI Paradigms
Simple parallel programs in MPI/PVM environments
Parallel algorithms on network
Addition of Matrices
Multiplication of Matrices
Parallel Programming Issues
Systolic Array

PARALLEL VIRTUAL MACHINE (PVM)

PVM is a portable message passing system, designed to connect separate heterogeneous host machines to form a single virtual machine. It is a single manageable parallel computing resource. Large computational problems like superconductivity studies, molecular dynamics simulations, and matrix algorithms can be solved more cost effectively by using the memory and the aggregate power of many computers. It manages all message routing, data conversion, task scheduling in the network of incompatible computer architectures.

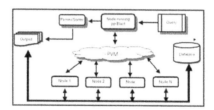

PVM (Parallel Virtual Machine) is a software system that enables a collection of heterogeneous computers to be used as a coherent and flexible concurrent computational resource.

The individual computers may be shared- or local-memory multiprocessors, vector supercomputers, specialized graphics engines, or scalar workstations, that may be interconnected by a variety of networks, such as ethernet, FDDI.

User programs written in C, C++ or Fortran access PVM through library routines (libpvm3.a and libfpvm3.a).

Daemon programs (pvmd3) provide communication and process control between computers.

Underlying principles

> • User-configured host-pool. The user selects the machines that will form the virtual parallel machine on which an application will run. The host-pool may be altered by adding and deleting

machines during operation.

- Translucent access to hardware. Application programs either may view the hardware environment as an attributeless collection of virtual processing elements or may choose to exploit the capabilities of specific machines in the host pool by positioning certain computational tasks on the most appropriate machines.

- Process-based computation. The unit of parallelism in PVM is a task, an independent sequential thread of control which alternates between computation and communication.

- Explicit message-passing model. Collections of tasks, each performing a part of an application's workload using data-, functional-, or hybrid decomposition, cooperate by explicitly sending and receiving messages to one another.

- Heterogeneity support. The PVM system supports heterogeneity in terms of machines, networks, and applications.
- Multiprocessor support. PVM uses the native message-passing facilities on multiprocessors to take advantage of the underlying hardware. Vendors sometimes supply their own optimized PVM for their architecture, which can still communicate with the public PVM version.

Structure of PVM

PVM is consists of two parts. The first part is a daemon, called pvmd3, that resides on all the computers making up the virtual machine. This daemon is constructed in such a way that every user can start it. Multiple users can use and configure different virtual machines simultaneously and each user can execute several PVM application simultaneously.

The second part of PVM is a library of PVM interface routines. This library contains user-callable routines for message-passing, spawning processes, coordinating tasks, and modifying the virtual machine.

Language bindings

The PVM system currently supports C, C++, and FORTRAN (77) language bindings. Wrappers for calling PVM from Fortran90 exist (see http://www.netlib.org/pvm).

Features of PVM

- Very easy to install and configure;
- Multiple users can use PVM at the same time;
- One user can execute multiple applications;
- It's a small package;
- Supports C, C++, Fortran;
- For a given run of a PVM program, users can select the group of machines;
- It is a message-passing model,
- Process-based computation;
- Supports heterogeneous architecture.

PVM3 (Parallel Virtual Machine, version 3) is a message passing library, to be used in Fortran and C programs. PVM3 is developed at Oak Ridge National Laboratory. The programming model is relatively easy to master and flexible. Creation and destruction of processes is under program control. PVM3 programs are easily portable to other hardware and operating systems, including Windows. With PVM3 it is possible to run parallel programs on collections of heterogeneous computer systems (for example:

one process could run on a NT machine, another one on the Cray supercomputer and some more processes on the RS/6000 SP). The number of processes per processor is unlimited, so the code can be developed, tested and debugged interactively using only one processor.

PVM3 is suitable for implementing data parallel and function parallel paradigms. The source code for PVM3 is freely obtainable from *http://w***ww.epm.ornl.gov/pvm/.**

Examples

Here are examples of simple PVM3 programs, (C and Fortran). Download the file pvm3-examples.tgz and issue the following command:

$ tar zxvf pvm3-examples.tgz

The Message Passing Model

MPI is intended as a standard implementation of the "message passing" model of parallel computing.

A parallel computation consists of a number of **processes**, each working on some local data. Each process has purely local variables, and there is no mechanism for any process to **directly** access the memory of another.

Sharing of data between processes takes place by message passing, that is, by explicitly sending and receiving data between processes.

Note that the model involves **processes**, which need not, in principle, be running on different **processors**. In this course, it is generally assumed that different processes are running on different processors and the terms "processes" and "processors" are used interchangeably (e.g., by speaking of processors communicating with one another).

A primary reason for the usefulness of this model is that it is extremely general. Essentially, any type of parallel computation can be cast in the message passing form. In addition, this model can be implemented on a wide variety of platforms, from shared-memory multiprocessors to networks of workstations and even single-processor machines generally allows more control over data location and flow within a parallel application than in, for example, the shared memory model. Thus programs can often achieve higher performance using explicit message passing. Indeed, performance is a primary reason why message passing is unlikely to ever disappear from the parallel programming world.

What is MPI?

MPI stands for "Message Passing Interface". It is a library of functions (in C) or subroutines (in Fortran) that you insert into source code to perform data communication between processes.

MPI was developed over two years of discussions led by the MPI Forum, a group of roughly sixty people representing some forty organizations.

The MPI-1 standard was defined in Spring of 1994.

This standard specifies the names, calling sequences, and results of subroutines and functions to be called from Fortran 77 and C, respectively. All implementations of MPI must conform to these rules, thus ensuring portability. MPI programs should compile and run on any platform that supports the MPI standard.

The detailed implementation of the library is left to individual vendors, who are thus free to produce optimized versions for their machines.
Implementations of the MPI-1 standard are available for a wide variety of platforms.

An MPI-2 standard has also been defined. It provides for additional features not present in MPI-1, including tools for parallel I/O, C++ and Fortran 90 bindings, and dynamic process management. At present, some MPI implementations include portions of the MPI-2 standard but the full MPI-2 is not yet available.

Goals of MPI

The primary goals addressed by MPI are to
- Provide source code portability. MPI programs should compile and run as-is on any platform.
- Allow efficient implementations across a range of architectures.

MPI also offers
A great deal of functionality, including a number of different types of communication, special routines for common "collective" operations, and the ability to handle user-defined data types and topologies.
Support for heterogeneous parallel architectures.

Some things that are explicitly outside the scope of MPI-1 are
The precise mechanism for launching an MPI program. In general, this is platform-dependent and you will need to consult your local documentation to find out how to do this.
Dynamic process management, that is, changing the number of processes while the code is running.
Debugging
Parallel I/O
Several of these issues are addressed in MPI-2.

Why (Not) Use MPI?

You should use MPI when you need to
Write **portable** parallel code.
Achieve high performance in parallel programming, e.g. when writing parallel libraries.
Handle a problem that involves irregular or dynamic data relationships that do not fit well into the "data-parallel" model.

You should not use MPI when you
Can achieve sufficient performance and portability using a data-parallel (e.g., High-Performance Fortran) or shared-memory approach (e.g., OpenMP, or proprietary directive-based paradigms).
Can use a pre-existing library of parallel routines (which may themselves be written using MPI).
Don't need parallelism at all!

Basic Features of Message Passing Programs

Message passing programs consist of multiple instances of a serial program that communicate by library calls. These calls may be roughly divided into four classes:
- Calls used to initialize, manage, and finally terminate communications.
- Calls used to communicate between pairs of processors.
- Calls that perform communications operations among groups of processors.
- Calls used to create arbitrary data types.

The first class of calls consists of calls for starting communications, identifying the number of processors being used, creating subgroups of processors, and identifying which processor is running a particular instance of a program.

The second class of calls, called point -to-point communications operations, consists of different types of send and receive operations.

The third class of calls is the collective operations that provide synchronization or certain types of well-defined communications operations among groups of processes and calls that perform communication/calculation operations.

The final class of calls provides flexibility in dealing with complicated data structures.

The following sections of this chapter will focus primarily on the calls from the second and third classes: point-to-point communications and collective operations.

A First Program: Hello World! –hello.c
C:

```
/*The Parallel Hello World Program*/
#include <stdio.h>
#include <mpi.h>

main(int argc, char **argv)
{
  int node;

  MPI_Init(&argc,&argv);
  MPI_Comm_rank(MPI_COMM_WORLD, &node);

  printf("Hello World from Node %d\n",node);

  MPI_Finalize();
}
```

In a nutshell, this program sets up a communication group of processes, where each process gets its rank, prints it, and exits. It is important for you to understand that in MPI, this program will start simultaneously on all machines. For example, if we had ten machines, then *running this program* would mean that ten separate instances of this program would start running together on ten different machines. This is a fundamental difference from ordinary C programs, where, when someone said ``run the program'', it was assumed that there was only one instance of the program running.

The first line,

#include <stdio>
should be familiar to all C programmers. It includes the standard input/output routines like **printf**.

The second line,
#include <mpi.h>
includes the MPI functions. The file **mpi.h** contains prototypes for all the MPI routines in this program; this file is located in /usr/local/mpi/include/mpi.h in case you actually want to look at it.

The program starts with the **main...** line which takes the usual two arguments **argc** and **argv**, and the program declares one integer variable, **node**. The first step of the program,

MPl_Init(&argc,&argv);

calls MPl_Init to initialize the MPI environment, and generally set up everything. This should be the first command executed in all programs. This routine takes pointers to argc and argv, looks at them, pulls out the purely MPI-relevant things, and generally fixes them so you can use command line arguments as normal.

Next, the program runs MPl_Comm_rank, passing it an address to **node**.

MPl_Comm_rank(MPl_COMM_WORLD, &node);

MPl_Comm_rank will set **node** to the rank of the machine on which the program is running. Remember that in reality, several instances of this program start up on several different machines when this program is run. These processes will each receive a unique number from MPl_Comm_rank.

Because the program is running on multiple machines, each will execute not only all of the commands thus far explained, but also the *hello world* message printf, which includes their own rank.

printf("Hello World from Node %d\n",node);

If the program is run on four computers, **printf** is called four times on four different machines simultaneously. The order in which each process executes the message is undetermined, based on when they each reach that point in their execution of the program, and how they travel on the network. Your guess is as good as mine. So, the four messages will get dumped to your screen in some undetermined order, such as:

Hello World from Node 2
Hello World from Node 0
Hello World from Node 3
Hello World from Node 1

Note that all the printf's, though they come from different machines, will send their output intact to your shell window; this is generally true of output commands. Input commands, like scanf, will only work on the process with rank zero.

After doing everything else, the program calls MPl_Finalize, which generally terminates everything and shuts down MPI. This should be the last command executed in all programs.

Fortran:

```
PROGRAM hello
    INCLUDE 'mpif.h'
    INTEGER err
    CALL MPl_INIT(err)
    PRINT *, "Hello world!"
    CALL MPl_FINALIZE(err)
END
```

For the moment note from the example that
    MPI functions/subroutines have names that begin with **MPl_**.
    There is an MPI header file (mpi.h or mpif.h) containing definitions and function prototypes
        that is imported via an "include" statement.

To compile this code, type:
    $mpicc -o hello hello.c
    or
    $mpif77 -o hello hello.f
To run this compiled code, type:
    $mpirun -np 4 hello

Assuming that we are on linux
You need to install MPI package - mpich, openMPI - use any package provided by your Linux package installer/repository (yum, apt-get,....).

Using mpicc, we can compile mpi code. We can use following command for compilation
mpicc filename.c

Using mpiexec (or mpirun), we can execute this code. We can use following command for executing(executable is a.out) it with 4 processes.
$mpiexec -np 4 ./a.out

Point-to-Point Communications and Messages

The elementary communication operation in MPI is "point-to-point" communication, that is, direct communication between two processors, one of which **sends** and the other **receives**.

Point-to-point communication in MPI is "two-sided", meaning that both an explicit send and an explicit receive are required. Data are not transferred without the participation of both processors.

In a generic send or receive, a **message** consisting of some block of data is transferred between processors. A message consists of an **envelope**, indicating the source and destination processors, and a **body**, containing the actual data to be sent.

MPI uses three pieces of information to characterize the message body in a flexible way:

Buffer* - the starting location in memory where outgoing data is to be found (for a send) or incoming data is to be stored (for a receive).

Datatype - the type of data to be sent. In the simplest cases this is an elementary type such as float/REAL, int/INTEGER, etc. In more advanced

applications this can be a user-defined type built from the basic types. These can be thought of as roughly analogous to C structures, and can contain data located anywhere, i.e., not necessarily in contiguous memory locations. This ability to make use of user-defined types allows complete flexibility in defining the message content.

Count - the number of items of type datatype to be sent.

Note that MPI standardizes the designation of the elementary types. This means that you don't have to explicitly worry about differences in how machines in heterogeneous environments represent them, e.g., differences in representation of floating-point numbers.

In C, **buffer** is the actual address of the array element where the data transfer begins. In Fortran, it is just the name of the array element where the data transfer begins. (Fortran actually gets the address behind the scenes.)

Communication Modes and Completion Criteria

MPI provides a great deal of flexibility in specifying how messages are to be sent. There are a variety of **communication modes** that define the procedure used to transmit the message, as well as a set of criteria for determining when the communication event (i.e., a particular send or receive) is **complete**. For example, a **synchronous send** is defined to be complete when receipt of the message at its destination has been acknowledged. A **buffered send**, however, is complete when the outgoing data has been copied to a (local) buffer; nothing is implied about the arrival of the message at its destination. In all cases, completion of a send implies that it is safe to overwrite the memory areas where the data were originally stored.

There are four communication modes available for sends:

1. Standard
2. Synchronous
3. Buffered
4. Ready

For receives there is only a single communication mode. A receive is complete when the incoming data has actually arrived and is available for use.

➤ **Blocking and Nonblocking Communication**
➤ **Blocking and Nonblocking Communication**

In addition to the communication mode used, a send or receive may be **blocking** or **nonblocking**.

A **blocking** send or receive does not return from the subroutine call until the operation has actually completed. Thus it insures that the relevant completion criteria have been satisfied before the calling process is allowed to proceed.

> With a blocking send, for example, you are sure that the variables sent can safely be overwritten on the sending processor. With a blocking receive, you are sure that the data has actually arrived and is ready for use.

A **nonblocking** send or receive returns immediately, with no information about whether the completion criteria have been satisfied. This has the advantage that the processor is free to do other things while the communication proceeds "in the background." You can test later to see whether the operation has actually completed.

> For example, a nonblocking synchronous send returns immediately, although the send will not be complete until receipt of the message has been acknowledged. The sending processor can then do other useful work, testing later to see if the send is complete. Until it is complete, however, you can not assume that the message has been received or that the variables to be sent may be safely overwritten.

Collective Communications

In addition to point-to-point communications between individual pairs of processors, MPI includes routines for performing **collective communications**. These routines allow larger groups of processors to communicate in various ways, for example, one-to-several or several-to-one.

The main advantages of using the collective communication routines over building the equivalent out of point-to-point communications are

The possibility of error is significantly reduced. One line of code -- the call to the collective routine -- typically replaces several point-to-point calls.

The source code is much more readable, thus simplifying code debugging and maintenance.

Optimized forms of the collective routines are often faster than the equivalent operation expressed in terms of point-to-point routines.

Examples of collective communications include **broadcast operations**, **gather and scatter operations**, and **reduction operations**. These are briefly described in the following two sections.

Broadcast Operations

The simplest kind of collective operation is the **broadcast**. In a broadcast operation a single process sends a copy of some data to all the other processes in a group. This operation is illustrated graphically in the figure below. Each row in the figure represents a different process. Each colored block in a column represents the location of a piece of the data. Blocks with the same color that are located on multiple processes contain copies of the same data.

Gather and Scatter Operations

Perhaps the most important classes of collective operations are those that distribute data from one processor onto a group of processors or vice versa. These are called **scatter** and **gather** operations. MPI provides two kinds of scatter and gather operations, depending upon whether the data can be evenly distributed across processors. These scatter and gather operations are illustrated below.

In a scatter operation, all of the data (an array of some type) are initially collected on a single processor (the left side of the figure). After the scatter operation, pieces of the data are distributed on different processors (the right side of the figure). The multicolored box reflects the possibility that the data may not be evenly divisible across the processors. The gather operation is the inverse operation to scatter: it collects pieces of the data that are distributed across a group of processors and reassembles them in the proper order on a single processor.

Reduction Operations

A **reduction** is a collective operation in which a single process (the **root** process) collects data from the other processes in a group and combines them into a single data item. For example, you might use a reduction to compute the sum of the elements of an array that is distributed over several processors. Operations other than arithmetic ones are also possible, for example, maximum and minimum, as well as various logical and bitwise operations.

Sample Program in MPI/PVM Environment: Hello World!

In this modified version of the "Hello World" program, each processor prints its rank as well as the total number of processors in the communicator MPI_COMM_WORLD.

C:

```
#include <stdio.h>
#include <mpi.h>
void main (int argc, char *argv[])
{
int myrank, size;
MPI_Init(&argc, &argv);          /* Initialize MPI      */
MPI_Comm_rank(MPI_COMM_WORLD, &myrank);   /* Get my rank */
```

```
MPI_Comm_size(MPI_COMM_WORLD, &size);        /* Get the total        number of processors */

printf("Processor %d of %d: Hello World!\n", myrank, size);
MPI_Finalize();/* Terminate MPI        */
}
```

Notes:
> Makes use of the pre-defined communicator MPI_COMM_WORLD.
> Not testing for error status of routines!

Hello World! mk. 2 (Fortran version)
Fortran:

```
   PROGRAM hello
      INCLUDE 'mpif.h'
      INTEGER myrank, size, ierr
C Initialize MPI:
      call MPI_INIT(ierr)

C Get my rank:
      call MPI_COMM_RANK(MPI_COMM_WORLD, myrank, ierr)
C Get the total number of processors:
      call MPI_COMM_SIZE(MPI_COMM_WORLD, size, ierr)
      PRINT *, "Processor", myrank, "of", size, ": Hello World!"
C Terminate MPI:
      call MPI_FINALIZE(ierr)
END
```

Notes:
> Makes use of the pre-defined communicator MPI_COMM_WORLD.
> Not testing for error status of routines!

Sample Program: Output

Running this code on four processors will produce a result like:

```
Processor 2 of 4: Hello World!
Processor 1 of 4: Hello World!
Processor 3 of 4: Hello World!
Processor 0 of 4: Hello World!
```

Each processor executes the same code, including probing for its rank and size and printing the string.
The order of the printed lines is essentially random!
> There is no intrinsic synchronization of operations on different processors.
> Each time the code is run, the order of the output lines may change.

Example: Send and Receive
In this program, process 0 sends a message to process 1, and process 1 receives it. Note the use of myrank in a conditional to limit execution of code to a particular process.

Fortran:
```
PROGRAM simple_send_and_receive
    INCLUDE 'mpif.h'
    INTEGER myrank, ierr, status(MPI_STATUS_SIZE)
    REAL a(100)
C Initialize MPI:
    call MPI_INIT(ierr)
C Get my rank:
    call MPI_COMM_RANK(MPI_COMM_WORLD, myrank, ierr)
C Process 0 sends, process 1 receives:
    if( myrank.eq.0 )then
        call MPI_SEND( a, 100, MPI_REAL, 1, 17, MPI_COMM_WORLD, ierr)
    else if ( myrank.eq.1 )then
        call MPI_RECV( a, 100, MPI_REAL, 0, 17, MPI_COMM_WORLD, status,
ierr ) endif
C Terminate MPI:
    call MPI_FINALIZE(ierr)
END
```

C:
```
/* simple send and receive */
#include <stdio.h>
#include <mpi.h>
void main (int argc, char **argv) {
  int    myrank;   MPI_Status    status;
  double a[100];

  MPI_Init(&argc, &argv); /* Initialize MPI */ MPI_Comm_rank(MPI_COMM_WORLD,
  &myrank); /* Get rank */ if( myrank == 0 ) /* Send a message */
    MPI_Send( a, 100, MPI_DOUBLE, 1, 17, MPI_COMM_WORLD );

  else if( myrank == 1 )  /* Receive a message */
    MPI_Recv( a, 100, MPI_DOUBLE, 0, 17, MPI_COMM_WORLD, &status );
  MPI_Finalize();                  /* Terminate MPI */
}
```

What Happens at Runtime

It is useful to keep in mind the following model for the runtime behavior of MPI_SEND. According to the model, when a message is sent using MPI_SEND one of two things may happen:

  The message may be copied into an MPI internal buffer and transferred to its destination later, in the background, or

  The message may be left where it is, in the program's variables, until the destination process is ready to receive it. At that time, the message is transferred to its destination.

The first option allows the sending process to move on to other things after the copy is completed. The second option minimizes copying and memory use, but may result in extra delay to the sending process. The delay can be significant.

Surprisingly, in 1., a call to MPI_SEND may return before any non-local action has been taken or even begun, i.e., before anything has happened that might naively be associated with sending a message. In 2., a synchronization between sender and receiver is implied.

MPI on Windows Platform: *MPICH2 on Code::Blocks*

Download Code::Blocks (*http://www.codeblocks.org/downloads/26#windows*) with mingw-setup.exe option.

Download MPICH (*http://www.mpich.org/static/downloads/1.4.1p1mpich2-1.4.1-win-ia32.msi/*)

MPICH, formerly known as MPICH2, is a freely available, portable implementation of MPI, a standard for message-passing for distributed-memory applications used in parallel computing. MPICH is Free and open source software with some public domain components that were developed by a US governmental organisation, and is available for Unix-like OS (including Linux and Mac OS X) as well as Windows.

I am using Windows 7 and I am assuming that before following these steps that you had already installed **Code::Blocks** and **MPICH2** (*mpich2-1.4.1p1-win-ia32.msi* from administrator login with everyone installation option)

Note that when you use Code::Blocks 32-bit you have to use also MPICH2 32-bit, even when your Windows is 64-bit.

So here now we go with the steps:

1. Add the MPICH2 bin path to you system variable "PATH":
    *   Right click "Computer" -> "Properties" -> "Advanced system settings" -> "Environment Variables..." -> click on "Path" and then Edit...

    *   Type your MPICH2 bin path at the beginning of the text, in my case "C:\Program Files\MPICH2\bin"

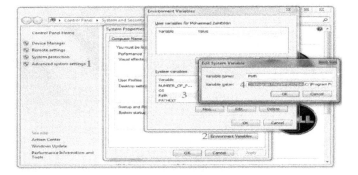

2. Open Code::Blocks, then click "Settings" -> "Compiler" (must be selected as GNU GCC)

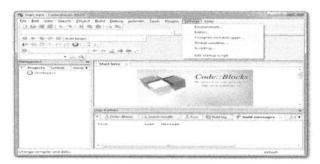

3. Click on "Linker settings" tab -> "Add" -> and then from the pop-up go to the MPICH2 installation directory and choose "lib\mpi.lib" -> then click "OK"

4. Click on "Search directories" tab -> "Add" -> and then from the pop-up go to the MPICH2 installation directory and choose "include" -> then click "OK"

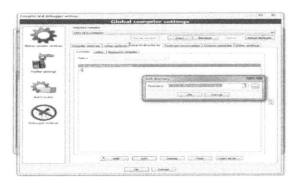

Now you can use Code::Blocks to write code using MPICH2 implementation, here is an example:

1. Open Code::Blocks (with GNU GCC Compiler option) and create new project:

- "File" -> "New" -> "Project..."
- choose "Console application" -> "Go"
- Follow the wizard to create a new project, you need to choose either "C" or "C++", then where to create your project... etc.

2. Open the "main.cpp" file and write the following code:

```
#include <iostream>
#include "mpi.h"
#include <string>
using namespace std;
int main(int argc, char *argv[])
{
    int my_rank;      /* rank of process */
    int noProcesses;  /* number of processes */
    int nameSize;     /* length of name */

    char computerName[MPI_MAX_PROCESSOR_NAME];

    MPI_Init(&argc, &argv); /*START MPI */

    /*Determines the size of the group associated with a communicator */
    MPI_Comm_size(MPI_COMM_WORLD, &noProcesses);

    /*Determines the rank of the calling process in the communicator*/
    MPI_Comm_rank(MPI_COMM_WORLD, &my_rank);

    /*Gets the name of the processor*/
```

```
MPI_Get_processor_name(computerName, &nameSize);

printf("Hello from process %d of %d processor on %s\n", my_rank, noProcesses,
computerName);

MPI_Finalize(); /* EXIT MPI */

return 0;
}
```

3. Build the code (Ctrl + F9), and then go the the directory where you saved your project, and then to "bin\Debug" of that particular directory.

Note: Select Settings->Debugger...->Full debug to have an exe file in bin\debug sub directory if there is an any issue.

4. To run the program open a Command Prompt, then type "**mpiexec -n 2 file.exe**" where:

- 2 is the number of processors to run the code on.
- "file.exe" the executable file that was generated in the "Debug" directory.

5. The output will be something like:
Hello from process 0 of 2 processor on accer-pc
Hello from process 1 of 2 processor on accer-pc

Note: Please specify an authentication passphrase for smpd: / Authentication Credential Issue then

1- Disable your Firewall (or modify the rules)

2- Open an admin command prompt by right-clicking on the command prompt icon selecting run as administrator.

3- Type the following commands on the prompt in sequence:
smpd -install
mpiexec -remove
mpiexec -register (this will ask for user name and password, enter it and confirm it)
mpiexec -validate (Must return SUCCESS)
smpd -status

The last command will return
'smpd running on hostname'
Every thing should work fine now.

Parallel Algorithms Underlying MPI Implementations

This chapter looks at a few of the parallel algorithms underlying the implementations of some simple MPI calls. The purpose of this is not to teach you how to "roll your own" versions of these routines, but rather to help you start thinking about algorithms in a parallel fashion. First, the method of **recursive halving and doubling**, which is the algorithm underlying operations such as broadcasts and reduction operations, is discussed. Then, specific examples of parallel algorithms that implement message passing are given.

Programming Based on Message Passing

As we know, the programming model based on message passing uses high level programming languages like C/C++ along with some message passing libraries like MPI and PVM. We had discussed MPI and PVM at great length in unit 2 on PRAM algorithms. Hence we are restricting ourselves to an example program of message passing.

Example 1: **Addition of array elements using two processors.**

In this problem, we have to find the sum of all the elements of an array A of size n. We shall divide n elements into two groups of roughly equal size. The first [n/2] elements are added by the first processor, P0 , and last [n/2] elements the by second processor, P1. The two sums then are added to get the final result. The program is given below:

Program for P0

```
#include <mpi.h>
#define n 100
int main(int argc, char **argv)
{
int A[n];
int sum0 =0, sum1=0,sum;
MPI_Init(&argc, &argv);
for( int i=0;i<n;i++)
scanf("%d", &A[i]);
MPI_Send( &n/2, n/2, MPI_INT,1, 0, MPI_COMM_WORLD);
for(i=1; i<n/2; i++)
sum0+=A[i];
sum1=MPI_Recv(&n/2, n/2, MPI_INT,1, 0, MPI_COMM_WORLD);
sum=sum0+sum1;
printf("%d",sum); MPI_Finalize();
}
```

Program for P1

```
int func( int B[int n])
{

MPI_Recv(&n/2, n/2, MPI_INT,0, 0, MPI_COMM_WORLD);
int sum1=0 ;
for (i=0; i</2; i++)
sum1+=B[i];
MPI_Send( 0, n/2, MPI_INT,0, 0, MPI_COMM_WORLD);
}
```

Recursive Halving and Doubling

To illustrate recursive halving and doubling, suppose you have a vector distributed among **p** processors, and you need the sum of all components of the vector in each processor, i.e., a sum reduction. One method is to use a tree-based algorithm to compute the sum to a single processor and then broadcast the sum to every processor.

Assume that each processor has formed the partial sum of the components of the vector that it has.

Step 1: Processor 2 sends its partial sum to processor 1 and processor 1 adds this partial sum to its own. Meanwhile, processor 4 sends its partial sum to processor 3 and processor 3 performs a similar summation.

Step 2: Processor 3 sends its partial sum, which is now the sum of the components on processors 3 and 4, to processor 1 and processor 1 adds it to its partial sum to get the final sum across all the components of the vector.

At each stage of the process, the number of processes doing work is cut in half. The algorithm is depicted in the Figure 13.1 below, where the solid arrow denotes a send operation and the dotted line arrow denotes a receive operation followed by a summation.

What about adding vectors? That is, how do you add several vectors component-wise to get a new vector? The answer is, you employ the method discussed earlier in a component-wise fashion. This fascinating way to reduce the communications and to avoid abundant summations is described next. This method utilizes the recursive halving and doubling technique and is illustrated in Figure 13.3 Suppose there are 4 processors and the length of each vector is also 4.

Step 1: Processor p0 sends the first two components of the vector to processor p1, and p1 sends the last two components of the vector to p0. Then p0 gets the partial sums for the last two components, and p1 gets the partial sums for the first two components. So do p2 and p3.

Step 2: Processor p0 sends the partial sum of the third component to processor p3. Processor p3 then adds to get the total sum of the third component. Similarly, processor 1, 2, and 4 find the total sums of the 4th, 2nd, and 1st components, respectively. Now the sum of the vectors are found and the components are stored in different processors.

Pseudocode for Broadcast Operation:

The following algorithm completes a broadcast operation in logarithmic time.
The first processor first sends the data to only two other processors. Then each of these processors send the data to two other processors, and so on. At each stage, the number of processors sending and receiving data doubles. The code is simple and looks similar to

```
if(myRank==0) {
    send to processors 1 and 2;
}
else
{
    receive from processors int((myRank-1)/2); torank1=2*myRank+1;
    torank2=2*myRank+2;
    if(torank1N)
```

```
        send to torank2;
}
```

The parallel algorithms in this chapter are presented in terms of one popular theoretical model: the parallel random-access machine, or PRAM (pronounced "PEE-ram"). Many parallel algorithms for arrays, lists, trees, and graphs can be easily described in the PRAM model. Although the PRAM ignores many important aspects of real parallel machines, the essential attributes of parallel algorithms tend to transcend the models for which they are designed. If one PRAM algorithm outperforms another PRAM algorithm, the relative performance is not likely to change substantially when both algorithms are adapted to run on a real parallel computer.

The PRAM model

The basic architecture of the *parallel random-access machine (PRAM)*. There are p ordinary (serial) processors $P_0, P_1, \ldots, P_{p}$1 that have as storage a shared, global memory. All processors can read from or write to the global memory "in parallel" (at the same time). The processors can also perform various arithmetic and logical operations in parallel.

The key assumption regarding algorithmic performance in the PRAM model is that running time can be measured as the number of parallel memory accesses an algorithm performs. This assumption is a straight- forward generalization of the ordinary RAM model, in which the number of memory accesses is asymptotically as good as any other measure of running time. This simple assumption will serve us well in our survey of parallel algorithms, even though real parallel computers cannot perform parallel accesses to global memory in unit time: the time for a memory access grows with the number of processors in the parallel computer.

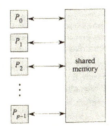

Figure: The basic architecture of the PRAM. There are p processors P_0, P_1, . . ., P_{p-1} connected to a shared memory. Each processor can access an arbitrary word of shared memory in unit time.

Nevertheless, for parallel algorithms that access data in an arbitrary fashion, the assumption of unit-time memory operations can be justified. Real parallel machines typically have a communication network that can support the abstraction of a global memory. Accessing data through the network is a relatively slow operation in comparison with arithmetic and other operations. Thus, counting the number of parallel memory accesses executed by two parallel algorithms does, in fact, yield a fairly accurate estimate of their relative performances. The principal way in which real machines violate the unit-time abstraction of the PRAM is that some memory-access patterns are faster than others. As a first approximation, however, the unit-time assumption in the PRAM model is quite reasonable.

127

The running time of a parallel algorithm depends on the number of processors executing the algorithm as well as the size of the problem input. Generally, therefore, we must discuss both time and processor count when analyzing PRAM algorithms; this contrasts with serial algorithms, in whose analysis we have focused mainly on time. Typically, there is a trade-off between the number of processors used by an algorithm and its running time.

Concurrent versus exclusive memory accesses

A *concurrent-read* algorithm is a PRAM algorithm during whose execution multiple processors can read from the same location of shared memory at the same time. An *exclusive-read* algorithm is a PRAM algorithm in which no two processors ever read the same memory location at the same time. We make a similar distinction with respect to whether or not multiple processors can write into the same memory location at the same time, dividing PRAM algorithms into *concurrent-write* and *exclusive-write* algorithms. Commonly used abbreviations for the types of algorithms we encounter are

◆*EREW*: exclusive read and exclusive write,

◆*CREW*: concurrent read and exclusive write,

◆*ERCW*: exclusive read and concurrent write, and

◆*CRCW*: concurrent read and concurrent write.

(These abbreviations are usually pronounced not as words but rather as strings of letters.)

Of these types of algorithms, the extremes--EREW and CRCW--are the most popular. A PRAM that supports only EREW algorithms is called an *EREW PRAM*, and one that supports CRCW algorithms is called a *CRCW PRAM*. A CRCW PRAM can, of course, execute EREW algorithms, but an EREW PRAM cannot directly support the concurrent memory accesses required in CRCW algorithms. The underlying hardware of an EREW PRAM is relatively simple, and therefore fast, because it needn't handle conflicting memory reads and writes. A CRCW PRAM requires more hardware support if the unit-time assumption is to provide a reasonably accurate measure of algorithmic performance, but it provides a programming model that is arguably more straightforward than that of an EREW PRAM.

Of the remaining two algorithmic types--CREW and ERCW--more attention has been paid in the literature to the CREW. From a practical point of view, however, supporting concurrency for writes is no harder than supporting concurrency for reads. In this chapter, we shall generally treat an algorithm as being CRCW if it contains either concurrent reads or concurrent writes, without making further distinctions.

When multiple processors write to the same location in a CRCW algorithm, the effect of the parallel write is not well defined without additional elaboration. In this chapter, we shall use the *common-CRCW* model: when several processors write into the same memory location, they must all write a common (the same) value. There are several alternative types of PRAM's in the literature that handle this problem with a different assumption. Other choices include

◆*Arbitrary*: an arbitrary value from among those written is actually stored,

◆*Priority*: the value written by the lowest-indexed processor is stored, and

◆*Combining*: the value stored is some specified combination of the values written.

In the last case, the specified combination is typically some associative and commutative function such as addition (store the sum of all the values written) or maximum (store only the maximum value written).

Synchronization and control

PRAM algorithms must be highly synchronized to work correctly. How is this synchronization achieved? Also, the processors in PRAM algorithms must often detect termination of loop conditions that depend on the state of all processors. How is this control function implemented?

We won't discuss these issues extensively. Many real parallel computers employ a control network connecting the processors that helps with synchronization and termination conditions. Typically, the control network can implement these functions as fast as a routing network can implement global memory references.

For our purposes, it suffices to assume that the processors are inherently tightly synchronized. All processors execute the same statements at the same time. No processor races ahead while others are further back in the code. As we go through our first parallel algorithm, we shall point out where we assume that processors are synchronized.

For detecting the termination of a parallel loop that depends on the state of all processors, we shall assume that a parallel termination condition can be tested through the control network in $O(1)$ time. Some EREW PRAM models in the literature do not make this assumption, and the (logarithmic) time for testing the loop condition must be included in the overall running time.

Parallel Algorithm - Matrix Multiplication

A matrix is a set of numerical and non-numerical data arranged in a fixed number of rows and column. Matrix multiplication is an important multiplication design in parallel computation. Here, we will discuss the implementation of matrix multiplication on various communication networks like mesh and hypercube.

A similar, albeit naive, type of decomposition can be achieved for matrix-matrix multiplication, **A=B*C**. The figure below shows schematically how matrix-matrix multiplication of two 4x4 matrices can be decomposed into four independent vector-matrix multiplications, which can be performed on four different processors.

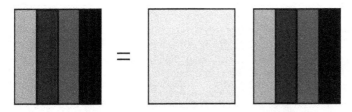

Figure 13.8. Schematic of a decomposition for matrix-matrix multiplication, **A=B*C**, in Fortran 90. The matrices **A** and **C** are depicted as multicolored columns with each color denoting a different processor. The matrix **B**, in yellow, is broadcast to all processors.

The basic steps are

Distribute the columns of **C** among the processors using a scatter operation.
Broadcast the matrix **B** to every processor.
Form the product of **B** with the columns of **C** on each processor. These are the

corresponding columns of **A**.
Bring the columns of **A** back to one processor using a gather operation.

The complete <u>Fortran 90 code</u> and <u>C code</u> are provided.

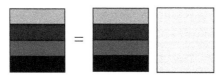

Figure 13.9. Schematic of a decomposition for matrix-matrix multiplication, **A=B*C**, in the C programming language. The matrices **A** and **B** are depicted as multicolored rows with each color denoting a different processor. The matrix **C**, in yellow, is broadcast to all processors.

Again, in C, the problem could be decomposed in rows. This is shown schematically below.

Mesh Network

A topology where a set of nodes form a p-dimensional grid is called a mesh topology. Here, all the edges are parallel to the grid axis and all the adjacent nodes can communicate among themselves.
Total number of nodes = (number of nodes in row) × (number of nodes in column)
A mesh network can be evaluated using the following factors –

- Diameter
- Bisection width

Diameter – In a mesh network, the longest **distance** between two nodes is its diameter. A p-dimensional mesh network having **kP** nodes has a diameter of **p(k−1)**.

Bisection width – Bisection width is the minimum number of edges needed to be removed from a network to divide the mesh network into two halves.

Matrix Multiplication Using Mesh Network

We have considered a 2D mesh network SIMD model having wraparound connections. We will design an algorithm to multiply two n × n arrays using n^2 processors in a particular amount of time.
Matrices A and B have elements a_{ij} and b_{ij} respectively. Processing element PE_{ij} represents a_{ij} and b_{ij}. Arrange the matrices A and B in such a way that every processor has a pair of elements to multiply. The elements of matrix A will move in left direction and the elements of matrix B will move in upward direction. These changes in the position of the elements in matrix A and B present each processing element, PE, a new pair of values to multiply.

Steps in Algorithm

- Stagger two matrices.
- Calculate all products, $a_{ik} \times b_{kj}$
- Calculate sums when step 2 is complete.

Algorithm
 Procedure MatrixMulti
 Begin

```
for k = 1 to n-1
for all Pij; where i and j ranges from 1 to n
if i is greater than k then
        rotate a in left direction
end if

if j is greater than k then
        rotate b in the upward direction
end if
for all Pij ; where i and j lies between 1 and n
        compute the product of a and b and store it in c
for k= 1 to n-1 step 1
for all Pi;j where i and j ranges from 1 to n
        rotate a in left direction
        rotate b in the upward direction
        c=c+aXb
End
```

CONCURRENTLY READ CONCURRENTLY WRITE (CRCW)

It is one of the models based on PRAM. In this model, the processors access the memory locations concurrently for reading as well as writing operations. In the algorithm, which uses CRCW model of computation, n3 number of processors are employed. Whenever a concurrent write operation is performed on a specific memory location, say m, than there are chances of occurrence of a conflict. Therefore, the write conflicts i.e. (WR, RW, WW) have been resolved in the following manner. In a situation when more than one processor tries to write on the same memory location, the value stored in the memory location is always the sum of the values computed by the various processors.

```
Algorithm Matrix Multiplication using CRCW
Input// Two Matrices M1 and M2
For I=1 to n     //Operation performed in PARALLEL
For j=1 to n  //Operation performed in PARALLEL
For k=1 to n //Operation performed in PARALLEL
Oij = 0;
Oij = M1ik * M2kj
End For
End For
End For
The complexity of CRCW based algorithm is O(1).
```

CONCURRENTLY READ EXCLUSIVELY WRITE (CREW)

It is one of the models based on PRAM. In this model, the processors access the memory location concurrently for reading while exclusively for writing operations. In the algorithm which uses CREW model of computation, n2 number of processors have been attached in the form of a two dimensional array of size n x n.

```
Algorithm Matrix Multiplication using CREW
Input// Two Matrices M1 and M2
For I=1 to n //Operation performed in PARALLEL For j=1 to n //Operation performed in PARALLEL
{
Oij = 0;
For k=1 to n
Oij = Oij + M1ik * M2kj End For
```

}
End For
End For
The complexity of CREW based algorithm is O(n).

Simulating a CRCW algorithm with an EREW algorithm

We now know that CRCW algorithms can solve some problems more quickly than can EREW algorithms. Moreover, any EREW algorithm can be executed on a CRCW PRAM. Thus, the CRCW model is strictly more powerful than the EREW model. But how much more powerful is it? A p-processor EREW PRAM can sort p numbers in $O(\lg p)$ time. We now use this result to provide a theoretical upper bound on the power of a CRCW PRAM over an EREW PRAM.

Theorem: A p-processor CRCW algorithm can be no more than $O(\lg p)$ times faster than the best p-processor EREW algorithm for the same problem.

Proof The proof is a simulation argument. We simulate each step of the CRCW algorithm with an $O(\lg p)$ -time EREW computation. Because the processing power of both machines is the same, we need only focus on memory accessing. We only present the proof for simulating concurrent writes here.

The p processors in the EREW PRAM simulate a concurrent write of the CRCW algorithm using an auxiliary array A of length p. Figure illustrates the idea. When CRCW processor P_i, for $i = 0, 1, \ldots, p - 1$, desires to write a datum x_i to a location l_i, each corresponding EREW processor P_i instead writes the ordered pair (l_i, x_i) to location $A[i]$. These writes are exclusive, since each processor writes to a distinct memory location. Then, the array A is sorted by the first coordinate of the ordered pairs in $O(\lg p)$ time, which causes all data written to the same location to be brought together in the output.

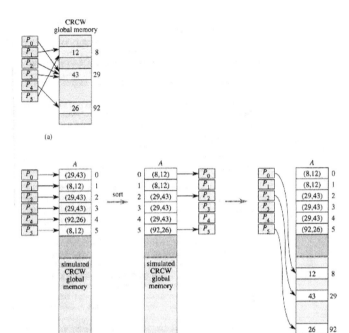

Figure: Simulating a concurrent write on an EREW PRAM.

(a) A step of a common-CRCW algorithm in which 6 processors write concurrently to global memory.

(b) Simulating the step on an EREW PRAM. First, ordered pairs containing location and data are written to an array A. The array is then sorted. By comparing adjacent elements in the array, we ensure that only the first of each group of identical writes into global memory is implemented. In this case, processors P_0, P_2, and P_5 perform the write.

Each EREW processor P_i, for $i = 1, 2, \ldots, p - 1$, now inspects $A[i] = (l_j, x_j)$ and $A[i - 1] = (l_k, x_k)$, where j and k are values in the range $0 \le j, k \le p - 1$. If $l_j \ne l_k$ or $i = 0$, then processor P_i, for $i = 0, 1, \ldots, p - 1$, writes the datum x_j to location l_j in global memory. Otherwise, the processor does nothing. Since the array A is sorted by first coordinate, only one of the processors writing to any given location actually succeeds, and thus the write is exclusive. This process thus implements each step of concurrent writing in the common-CRCW model in $O(\lg p)$ time.

The issue arises, therefore, of which model is preferable--CRCW or EREW--and if CRCW, which CRCW model. Advocates of the CRCW models point out that they are easier to program than the EREW model and that their algorithms run faster. Critics contend that hardware to implement concurrent memory operations is slower than hardware to implement exclusive memory operations, and thus the faster running time of CRCW algorithms is fictitious. In reality, they say, one cannot find the maximum of n values in $O(1)$ time.

Others say that the PRAM--either EREW or CRCW--is the wrong model entirely. Processors must be interconnected by a communication network, and the communication network should be part of the model. Processors should only be able to communicate with their neighbors in the network.

It is quite clear that the issue of the "right" parallel model is not going to be easily settled in favor of any one model. The important thing to realize, however, is that these models are just that: models. For a given real-world situation, the various models apply to differing extents. The degree to which the model matches the engineering situation is the degree to which algorithmic analyses in the model will predict real-world phenomena. It is important to study the various parallel models and algorithms, therefore, so that as the field of parallel computing grows, an enlightened consensus on which paradigms of parallel computing are best suited for implementation can emerge.

Parallel Programming Designing Issues

The main goal of writing a parallel program is to get better performance over the serial version. With this in mind, there are several designing issues that you need to consider when designing your parallel code to obtain the best performance possible within the constraints of the problem being solved. These issues are

Partitioning

One of the first steps in designing a parallel program is to break the problem into discrete "chunks" of work that can be distributed to multiple tasks. This is known as decomposition or partitioning. There are two basic ways to partition computational work among parallel tasks: **domain decomposition** and **functional decomposition**.

Domain Decomposition:

- In this type of partitioning, the data associated with a problem is decomposed. Each parallel task then works on a portion of the data.

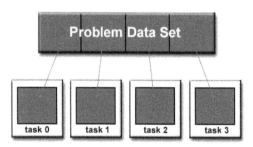

- There are different ways to partition data:

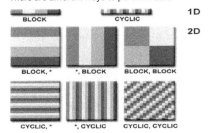

Functional Decomposition:
- In this approach, the focus is on the computation that is to be performed rather than on the data manipulated by the computation. The problem is decomposed according to the work that must be done. Each task then performs a portion of the overall work.
-

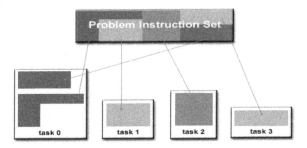

- Functional decomposition lends itself well to problems that can be split into different tasks. For example:
Ecosystem Modeling
Each program calculates the population of a given group, where each group's growth depends on that of its neighbors. As time progresses, each process calculates its current state, then exchanges information with the neighbor populations. All tasks then progress to calculate the state at the next time step.

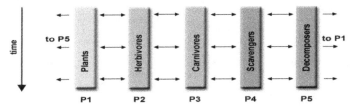

Communication

There are a number of important factors to consider when designing your program's inter-task communications:

- **Communication overhead**
  - o Inter-task communication virtually always implies overhead.
  - o Machine cycles and resources that could be used for computation are instead used to package and transmit data.
  - o Communications frequently require some type of synchronization between tasks, which can result in tasks spending time "waiting" instead of doing work.
  - o Competing communication traffic can saturate the available network bandwidth, further aggravating performance problems.

- **Latency vs. Bandwidth**
  - o *latency* is the time it takes to send a minimal (0 byte) message from point A to point B. Commonly expressed as microseconds.
  - o *bandwidth* is the amount of data that can be communicated per unit of time. Commonly expressed as megabytes/sec or gigabytes/sec.
  - o Sending many small messages can cause latency to dominate communication overheads. Often it is more efficient to package small messages into a larger message, thus increasing the effective communications bandwidth.

- **Visibility of communications**
  - o With the Message Passing Model, communications are explicit and generally quite visible and under the control of the programmer.
  - o With the Data Parallel Model, communications often occur transparently to the programmer, particularly on distributed memory architectures. The programmer may not even be able to know exactly how inter-task communications are being accomplished.

- **Synchronous vs. asynchronous communications**
  - o Synchronous communications require some type of "handshaking" between tasks that are sharing data. This can be explicitly structured in code by the programmer, or it may happen at a lower level unknown to the programmer.
  - o Synchronous communications are often referred to as *blocking* communications since other work must wait until the communications have completed.
  - o Asynchronous communications allow tasks to transfer data independently from one another. For example, task 1 can prepare and send a message to task 2, and then immediately begin doing other work. When task 2 actually receives the data doesn't matter.
  - o Asynchronous communications are often referred to as *non-blocking* communications since other work can be done while the communications are taking place.
  - o Interleaving computation with communication is the single greatest benefit for using asynchronous communications.

- **Scope of communications**
  - o Knowing which tasks must communicate with each other is critical during the design stage of a parallel code. Both of the two scopings described below can be implemented synchronously or asynchronously.
  - o *Point-to-point* - involves two tasks with one task acting as the sender/producer of data, and the other acting as the receiver/consumer.
  - o *Collective* - involves data sharing between more than two tasks, which are often specified as being members in a common group, or collective. Some common variations (there are more):

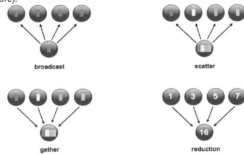

- **Efficiency of communications**
  - o Oftentimes, the programmer has choices that can affect communications performance. Only a few are mentioned here.
  - o Which implementation for a given model should be used? Using the Message Passing Model as an example, one MPI implementation may be faster on a given hardware platform than another.
  - o What type of communication operations should be used? As mentioned previously, asynchronous communication operations can improve overall program performance.
  - o Network fabric - some platforms may offer more than one network for communications. Which one is best?
  - o
- **Overhead and Complexity**

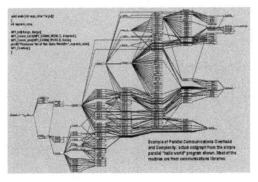

Example of Parallel Communications Overhead and Complexity: actual callgraph from the simple parallel "hello world" program shown. Most of the routines are from communications libraries.

- Finally, realize that this is only a partial list of things to consider!!!

Synchronization

Managing the sequence of work and the tasks performing it is a critical design consideration for most parallel programs.
Can be a significant factor in program performance (or lack of it)
Often requires "serialization" of segments of the program.

Types of Synchronization:

- **Barrier**

  - Usually implies that all tasks are involved
  - Each task performs its work until it reaches the barrier. It then stops, or "blocks".
  - When the last task reaches the barrier, all tasks are synchronized.
  - What happens from here varies. Often, a serial section of work must be done. In other cases, the tasks are automatically released to continue their work.

- **Lock / semaphore**

  - Can involve any number of tasks
  - Typically used to serialize (protect) access to global data or a section of code. Only one task at a time may use (own) the lock / semaphore / flag.
  - The first task to acquire the lock "sets" it. This task can then safely (serially) access the protected data or code.
  - Other tasks can attempt to acquire the lock but must wait until the task that owns the lock releases it.
  - Can be blocking or non-blocking

- **Synchronous communication operations**

  - Involves only those tasks executing a communication operation
  - When a task performs a communication operation, some form of coordination is required with the other task(s) participating in the communication. For example, before a task can perform a send operation, it must first receive an acknowledgment from the receiving task that it is OK to send.
  - Discussed previously in the Communications section.

Data Dependencies

A *dependence* exists between program statements when the order of statement execution affects the results of the program.

A *data dependence* results from multiple use of the same location(s) in storage by different tasks.
- Dependencies are important to parallel programming because they are one of the primary inhibitors to parallelism.

138

Examples:
- **Loop carried data dependence**

```
DO J = MYSTART,MYEND
    A(J) = A(J-1) * 2.0
END DO
```

The value of A(J-1) must be computed before the value of A(J), therefore A(J) exhibits a data dependency on A(J-1). Parallelism is inhibited.
If Task 2 has A(J) and task 1 has A(J-1), computing the correct value of A(J) necessitates:
  - o   Distributed memory architecture - task 2 must obtain the value of A(J-1) from task 1 after task 1 finishes its computation
  - o   Shared memory architecture - task 2 must read A(J-1) after task 1 updates it
- **Loop independent data dependence**

```
task 1      task 2
------      ------

X = 2      X = 4
  .          .
  .          .
Y = X**2   Y = X**3
```

As with the previous example, parallelism is inhibited. The value of Y is dependent on:
  - o   Distributed memory architecture - if or when the value of X is communicated between the tasks.
  - o   Shared memory architecture - which task last stores the value of X.
- Although all data dependencies are important to identify when designing parallel programs, loop carried dependencies are particularly important since loops are possibly the most common target of parallelization efforts.

How to Handle Data Dependencies:

- Distributed memory architectures - communicate required data at synchronization points.
- Shared memory architectures -synchronize read/write operations between tasks.

Load Balancing

Load balancing refers to the practice of distributing approximately equal amounts of work among tasks so that *all* tasks are kept busy *all* of the time. It can be considered a minimization of task idle time.
Load balancing is important to parallel programs for performance reasons. For example, if all tasks are subject to a barrier synchronization point, the slowest task will determine the overall performance.

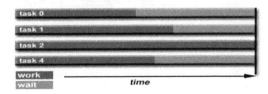

How to Achieve Load Balance:

- **Equally partition the work each task receives**
  - o For array/matrix operations where each task performs similar work, evenly distribute the data set among the tasks.
  - o For loop iterations where the work done in each iteration is similar, evenly distribute the iterations across the tasks.
  - o If a heterogeneous mix of machines with varying performance characteristics are being used, be sure to use some type of performance analysis tool to detect any load imbalances. Adjust work accordingly.
- **Use dynamic work assignment**
  - o Certain classes of problems result in load imbalances even if data is evenly distributed among tasks:

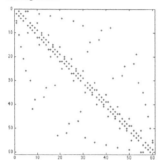 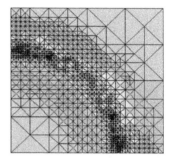

Sparse arrays - some tasks will have actual data to work on while others have mostly "zeros".

Adaptive grid methods - some tasks may need to refine their mesh while others don't.

  - o When the amount of work each task will perform is intentionally variable, or is unable to be predicted, it may be helpful to use a ***scheduler-task pool*** approach. As each task finishes its work, it receives a new piece from the work queue.

  - o Ultimately, it may become necessary to design an algorithm which detects and handles load imbalances as they occur dynamically within the code.

Debugging

- Debugging parallel codes can be incredibly difficult, particularly as codes scale upwards.
- The good news is that there are some excellent debuggers available to assist:
  - o Threaded - pthreads and OpenMP
  - o MPI
  - o GPU / accelerator

- o Hybrid
- Livermore Computing users have access to several parallel debugging tools installed on LC's clusters:
  - o TotalView from RogueWave Software
  - o DDT from Allinea
  - o Inspector from Intel
  - o Stack Trace Analysis Tool (STAT) - locally developed
- All of these tools have a learning curve associated with them - some more than others.

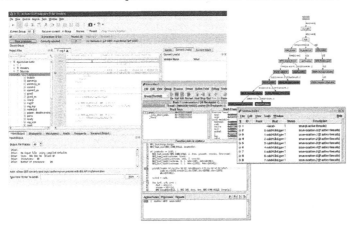

The term SYSTOLIC ARRAY

The term systolic array was introduced in the computer science by H. T. Kung at the end of 70's. A systolic array typically consists of a large number of similar processing elements interconnected in an array. The interconnections are local meaning that each processing element can communicate only with a limited number of neighbouring processing elements. Data move at a constant velocity through the systolic array passing from one processing element to the next processing element. Each of the processing elements performs computations, thus contributing to the overall processing needed to be done by the array.

Systolic arrays are synchronous systems. A global clock synchronises the exchange of data between directly communicating processing elements. Data can be exchanged only at the ticks of the clock. Between two consecutive clock ticks, each processing element carries out computation on the data which it has received upon the last tick and produces data which is sent to neighbouring processing elements at the next clock tick. The processing element can also hold data stored in the local memory of the processing element.

A data flow, which moves through systolic array, resembles the pulsing movement of the blood under contractions of the heart, which are called *systoles* in physiology (Figure 5). This analogy was the reason to give such computing structures the attribute systolic .

Figure:: Analogy of data movement in a systolic array with the pulsing movement of the blood.

Another explanation of the systolic term is connected with the overall system in which the systolic array plays a role of co-processor. A host computer supplies the systolic array with data and extracts the data, which has been processed, by the systolic array. The system resembles the blood circulatory system, in that the host pumps data through systolic array like the heart, which pumps blood through the arteries, capillaries and veins (Figure 6).

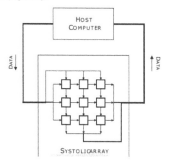

Figure 6: Analogy of the computing system with the blood circulatory system

Features of systolic arrays

There are several similar definitions of systolic arrays. According to Kung and Leiserson, we have the following well known definition:

"A systolic system is a network of processors which rhythmically compute and pass data through the system."

A more consistent definition of systolic arrays is presented below. A systolic array is a computing system, which possesses the following features]:

Network. It is computing network employing a number of processing elements (PEs)[3] or cells with interconnections.

Rhythm. The data are computed and passed through the network in a rhythmic and continual manner.

Synchrony. A global clock times the execution of instructions and the communication data.

Modularity. The network consists of one or, at most, a few types of processing elements. If there is more than one type of processors, the systolic array can usually be decomposed into distinct parts with one processor type.

Regularity. The interconnections between the processing elements are regular and homogeneous. The numbers of interconnections for processing elements are independent on the problem size.

Locality. The interconnections are local. Only neighbouring processing elements can communicate directly.

Boundary. Only boundary processing elements in the network communicate with the outside world.

Extensibility. The computing network may be extended indefinitely.

Pipelinebility. All data is proceeded and transferred by pipelining. As presented in the sequel, it means that at least one delay element (register) is present between each two directly connected combinatorial PEs.

From the features presented above we can summarise that a large number of PEs work in parallel on different parts of the computational problem. Data enter the systolic array at the boundary. Once input into the systolic array, data is used many times before it is output. In general, several data flows move at constant velocities through the array and interact with each other during this movement, where processing elements execute repeatedly one and the same function. There is no transfer of intermediate results from the array to the host computer. Only initial data and final results are transferred between the host and the systolic array.

As long as VLSI technology is used, certain constraints should be analysed and incorporated in the design methodology. A few, most important, are short communication paths, limited input/output interaction, time consuming data transfer and synchronisation. These constraints are all incorporated in the above features of the systolic array. Features like regularity, modularity and locality are especially favourable from the VLSI point of view and make systolic arrays good candidates for the VLSI implementation.

Formal representation of systolic arrays

The systolic arrays are usually represented as array of processing elements and array of interconnections connecting the PEs with some particular pattern. In other words, systolic array is a collection of PEs that are arranged in a particular pattern. The pattern and the PEs are defined with the implemented algorithm.

The PEs are composed of combinatorial part and/or memory. The combinatorial part is responsible for arithmetic operations required by the systolic algorithm. By memory (registers) we denote delay elements within the PE that hold data and thus control data flow into and out of the PE. In general, no large memory is associated with PEs.

The PE can be formally defined as an abstract automaton. Automata notations are extensively used as a fundamental representation of different computing structures. Automata with processing capabilities and memory are models of basic data storage and transfer functions.

Figure 7: Automaton a) combinatorial automaton, b) delay element, c) automaton with internal variable (memory), and d) equivalent representation using delay element.

The automaton is in general a system that consists of *input, output* and *internal variables*. The functional behaviour of the automaton is usually described by the state equations that specify the values of its internal and output variables.[4] If the automaton does not contain an internal variable it is named a *combinatorial* automaton. And further, if the automaton merely delays the flow of the input data by one time step it is called *delay* element and thus presents a memory element.

Rippling, Broadcasting, Pipelining

The three important terms needed for the presentation of systolic mode of operation are presented next, namely rippling, broadcasting, and pipelining .

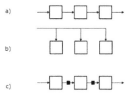

Figure 8: a) Rippling: the direct connection of combinatorial PEs results in rippling. b) Broadcasting: data is simultaneously input to the number of PEs via a common input. c) Pipelining: chaining of combinatorial PEs via delay elements.

Rippling occurs if combinatorial automata are directly connected. Since there is no delay elements data items propagate along the chain as a front of a wave. The next data item can only be input after the previous has exited the chain. Therefore the clock period is defined by the overall combinatorial delay of the chain.

Broadcasting is the case where a number of PEs receive the same signal from the common input line. This form of global data transfer is called broadcasting and is undesirable from VLSI implementation point of view, since long connections present long delay in fast clocked systems.

Pipelining is a contrast to rippling. The cells are chained via delay elements. A data item moves under the control of the clock from cell to cell. As a result the clock period is determined by the combinatorial delay of a single cell. In pipeline, a sequence of data items can be processed in parallel, as opposed to just one datum at a time in a rippling chain.

Parallel computing structures can be efficiently represented with the appropriate combination of many automata. In addition, if the automata are connected to certain neighbouring automata, the resulting structure is called *cellular* automaton. In cellular automaton, the delay elements serve to quantise the data flow in time steps.

Systolic automata can be considered as a special class of cellular automata. The systolic automaton is completely pipelined version of a cellular automaton. In addition, the PEs have equal combinatorial delay. The complete pipelining is achieved by introducing the delay element into each connection between two PEs of the systolic automaton. As a result the broadcasting is eliminated[5]. As mentioned, it is important that the PEs exhibit equal combinatorial delays. This restriction does not mean that the PEs must be of one type but rather that the PEs have comparable combinatorial delays. This guarantees a balanced load of the PEs. Otherwise the efficiency of the system would be dominated by its slowest component.

Systolic array is then defined in the context of systolic automata with an additional requirement that the PEs are of one type and regularly arranged and interconnected. The regularity of the structure is especially important from the VLSI implementation point of view. The regularity contains the arrangement of the PEs as well as the interconnections between them. The requirement of PEs of the same type is an advantage from economic as well as from programming point of view. The restriction to one type of PEs also results in equal combinatorial delay and load balancing.

Examples of systolic array structures

Linear systolic array

In a linear systolic array, processing elements are arranged in one-dimension. The inter-connections between the processing elements are nearest neighbour only. Linear systolic arrays differ relative to the number of data flows and their relative velocities. Representatives of linear systolic arrays are matrix-vector multiplication, one-dimensional convolution, etc..

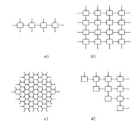

Figure 9: Examples of mesh-connected systolic structures. a) linear systolic array, b) orthogonal systolic array, c) hexagonal systolic array and d) triangular systolic array.

Orthogonal systolic array

In an orthogonal systolic array processing elements are arranged in a two-dimensional grid. Each processing element is interconnected to its nearest neighbours to the north, east, south and west. Again, the systolic arrays differ relative to the number and direction of data flows and the number of delay elements arranged in them. The most typical representative of this class is one of possible mappings of the matrix-matrix multiplication algorithm (0).

Hexagonal systolic array

In a hexagonal systolic array processing elements are arranged in a two-dimensional grid. The processing elements are connected with its nearest neighbours where inter-connections have hexagonal symmetry. A particular mapping of the matrix-matrix multiplication algorithm results in a hexagonal array].

Triangular systolic array

The term triangular systolic array refers to two-dimensional systolic array where processing elements are arranged in a triangular form. This topology is mostly used in different algorithms from linear algebra. In particular it is used in Gaussian elimination and other decomposition algorithms.

Thank You ....